Stopping the
WING-T
With the
4–3 Defense

BOB KENIG

Harding Press
Haworth, New Jersey 07641

*This book is lovingly dedicated to my wife, Sandy,
and our two wonderful daughters, Stacy and Shannon.*

Library of Congress Cataloging-in-Publication Data

Kenig, Bob
    Stopping the Wing-T with the 4–3 defense / Bob Kenig.
      p. cm.
    ISBN 1-890450-03-0 (paperback)
    1. Football—Defense—United States. 2. Football—Coaching—
United States. I. Title.
    GV951.18.K488   1999
    796.332'2—dc21
                                        98-43202
                                            CIP

ISBN 1-890450-03-0

Printed in the United States of America

HARDING PRESS
P. O. Box 141
Haworth, NJ 07641
hardingpress@earthlink.net

Books by and for the coaching profession

Contents

How This Book Will Help You

Defensing the Delaware Wing-T has been, and continues to be, a very popular book. However, it deals with the 3–4 defensive scheme. *Football's Modern 4–3 Defense*, another highly successful publication, deals only briefly with the dynamic Delaware Wing-T Offense. Since the use of the Wing-T, particularly in high schools, continues to grow and the 4–3 is still the most widely used defensive scheme in the NCAA, I decided it might be time for a new book. Numerous inquiries concerning how to stop the Wing-T with the 4–3 convinced me this book could be "just what the doctor ordered."

This book is concerned with stopping the Wing-T offense using the Basic 4–3 Defense and several 4–3 variations. Hopefully, you will have a basic knowledge of both the offense and the defense, as I did not go into, in great depth, many of the basics I previously covered in my other two volumes.

This manual is for the coach who wants to know the basics of using the 4–3 Defense against the common Wing-T plays. Several offensive formations are used throughout the book but, of course, the 4–3 can be successfully employed against all the various Wing-T formations. To illustrate the defense versus all the possible Wing-T formations and plays would take numerous volumes. However, the defensive principles described, in detail, in this text will definitely work versus all formation variations and plays.

If you have any questions or comments concerning this text or about our version of the 4–3 Defense, please feel free to contact me. I hope you enjoy reading this book as much as I enjoyed writing it.

Chapter 1

Installing the Basic 4–3 Defense

The 4–3 defensive package described in this book is the basic 4–3 package employed by many high school, college, and pro teams with minor variations. However, the adjustments and stunts presented are schemes our staff developed while employing the 4–3 Defense at Widener University, Delaware Valley College, and La Salle University.

Those who have read *Football's Modern 4–3 Defense* will notice that certain refinements and name changes have occurred in the defensive package since that book was originally introduced. Our 4–3 Defense changes and, hopefully, improves each season. A defensive or offensive scheme that remains unchanged from season to season is either perfect or is not totally evaluated at the end of each season. I have never been fortunate enough to coach a team with either a perfect offense or defense and, as a result, minor changes have occurred.

THE BASICS OF THE 4–3

Gap Descriptions

Every member of the defensive front is responsible for a gap along the line of scrimmage. This is true in the Base front as well as in all stunts and blitzes. For coaching purposes, and for ease of communication with the players, each gap is given a letter name. (Diagram 1-1)

DIAGRAM 1-1

Individual Alignments

Each member of the defensive front is given a landmark on which to align. Rather than instruct a defensive player to align on the outside shoulder, inside shoulder, or head on an offensive player, we divide each offensive player on or near the Line of Scrimmage (LOS) into three possible alignment landmarks. These landmarks are given number and, in several instances, number-letter names. (Diagram 1-2) When a player aligns on one of these areas, he is said to be aligning in that "technique." For example, when a player aligns on the "2" position, he is aligned in what is described as a "2 technique." It is imperative that each defensive lineman attack the offensive player on whom he is aligned. Without doing this, the offensive lineman has a "free shot" at a linebacker.

DIAGRAM 1-2

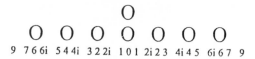

When a player aligns over one of these landmarks, a zero (0) is added to his alignment technique. For example, when the strongside outside linebacker (Sam) aligns over the 5 landmark and is off the ball, he is aligned in a "50 technique."

Positions

In the Base Defense, the front seven players align as follows:
- Strongside End (E) — 7 technique
- Strongside Tackle (T) — 3 technique
- Weakside Tackle (T) — 1 technique
- Weakside End (E) — 5 technique
- Strongside Linebacker (Sam) — 50 technique
- Middle Linebacker (Mike) — From 20i to 20i technique
- Weakside Linebacker (Will) — 50 technique

(Diagram 1-3)

Although these alignments are considered the Base alignments (techniques), we often put the T's in a 2 technique, the strong end in a 6 technique, and the weak end in a 4 technique. From these alignments, the four down linemen maintain their basic gap responsibilities. We often use these "Head-Up" alignments with our Stunt and Blitz package. This is one

DIAGRAM 1-3

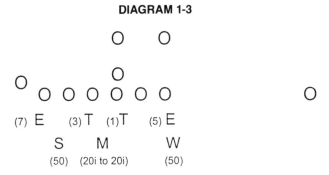

method of disguising our front. We can execute our Base from either our normal alignment or the Head-Up alignment. Although the stunts and blitzes used in this book are best executed from the Head-Up alignment, they can be, and often are, executed from our normal 4–3 alignment. This prohibits the offense from recognizing when a stunt or blitz is about to occur. (Diagram 1-4)

DIAGRAM 1-4

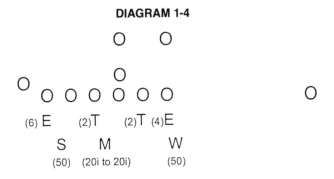

Formation Strength

The alignments of the defensive personnel are determined by the strength of the offensive formation. The Sam always goes to the strong side of the formation, and the Will goes to the weak side. The 7 and 3 techniques align to the strong side while the 1 and 5 techniques align to the weak side.

For the defensive front, the first criterion for the strength call is the tight end. No matter what kind of offensive formation is employed, as long as there is a tight end, the strength call is to his side.

Strength for the secondary, and for the front when there is no tight end, is the side of the formation with the most possible receivers on or near the LOS. In a formation with double split ends and a slot to one side, the strength call is to the slot side (two-receiver side). (Diagram 1-5) In a

DIAGRAM 1-5

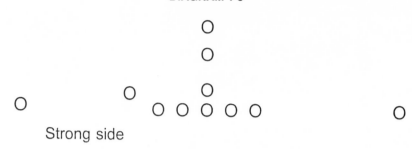

Strong side

balanced formation, with two receivers to either side and neither is a tight end, strength is determined by field position. If the ball is in the middle of the field, strength is to the defensive left. If the ball is on, or very near, a hash mark, strength is to the wide side of the field. (Diagram 1-6) In a balanced formation, with two receivers to either side and one side has a tight end, the strength call is to the tight-end side for the front and the secondary. (Diagram 1-7)

From a strength standpoint, we consider the basic wing and slot formations in the Wing-T offense as balanced sets with two receivers to

DIAGRAM 1-6

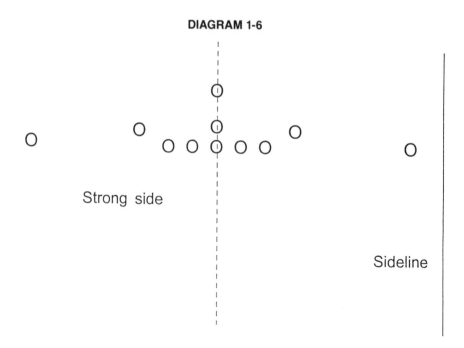

Strong side

Sideline

DIAGRAM 1-7

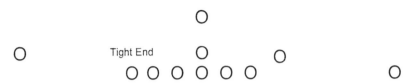

Strong side

either side of the formation. In the wing set, we treat the tight end and wing as two receivers. To the other side, the split end is a receiver, and the set halfback, because of the width of his alignment, is also considered a possible receiver. Since there is a tight end, the defensive front declares strength to the tight-end side. However, depending on scouting reports, down and distance, field position, and the tendency of the offense to use the Waggle to the split-end side, the secondary could, and often does, recognize the split-end side as the strong side. (Diagram 1-8)

The slot set presents a similar situation. The tight-end side, with the set halfback, is considered a two-receiver side and, since there is a tight end, the front declares that side as the strong side. The secondary recognizes the split-end/slot side, because it is a two-receiver side with one receiver split, as the strong side and declares strength there. (Diagram 1-9)

When the wing or slot executes normal Wing-T motion, the secondary strength may remain with the original call or change. This depends on scouting reports, down and distance, and field position.

DIAGRAM 1-8

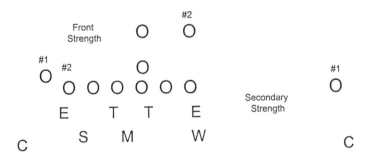

DIAGRAM 1-9

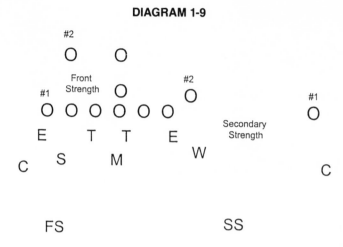

THREE-DEEP STRONG ZONE COVERAGE (GREEN)

Although we employ several different coverages while using the Base 4–3 front, for the purpose of simplicity and brevity the three-deep strong zone coverage is described in this book against the Wing-T Offense. We often use Green coverage with our Base front against the Wing-T, but we often employ other coverages as well.

Secondary Initial Alignment

Since disguise is a very big part of our defensive package, the secondary rarely aligns in a three-deep alignment. Normally, the secondary shows a four-deep "Umbrella Look," and the defenders move to their coverage responsibilities on the snap of the ball.

The corners (C) align 6 yards deep and 1 yard outside the widest receiver (#1) to their side. The safeties align 10 to 12 yards deep and split the distance between the number one and number two receivers to their side. The strong safety (SS) always goes to the strong side of the formation (two-receiver side) and the free safety (FS) goes opposite. (Diagram 1-10)

Secondary Assignments

The deep outside one-third strongside zone may be covered by either the C or the SS, depending on the width of the split of #1. Versus the normal Wing-T sets, C has responsibility for the zone when #1 is split more than 8 yards from the offensive tackle and the SS has the curl-to-flat responsibility to that side. This type of rotation occurs versus the slot/split-end side of the

DIAGRAM 1-10

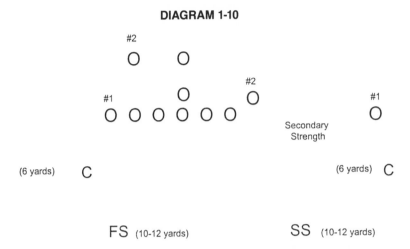

slot formation and the setback/split-end side of the wing formation when the secondary has declared those sides of the formations as strong. (Diagrams 1-11 and 1-12)

When the wing/tight-end side of the wing formation or the setback/tight-end side of the slot formation is declared as the strong side of these

DIAGRAM 1-11

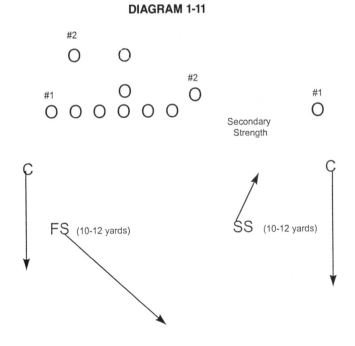

DIAGRAM 1-12

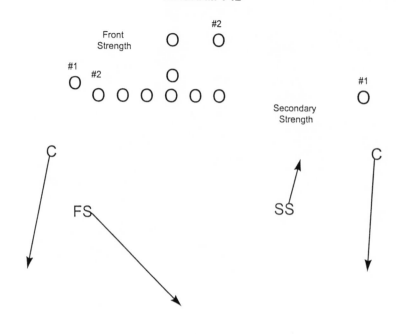

DIAGRAM 1-13

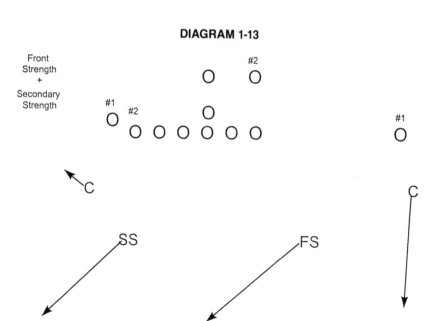

formations (rarely is the setback/tight-end side of the slot formation declared as the strong side), the C is responsible for the flat area and the SS covers the outside one-third zone. (Diagram 1-13)

The FS is always responsible for the deep middle one-third zone, while the other C covers the deep outside one-third weakside zone.

Linebacker Assignments

The Sam and Will have, primarily, the same assignments versus the pass. They are both responsible for the curl area. However, the outside linebacker to the weak side (determined by the secondary strength call) has no defender responsible for the flat area to his side. In a strong three-deep zone coverage, the vulnerable area is the weakside flat. This is certainly one reason why the coverage is disguised prior to the snap of the ball. The linebacker responsible for the weakside curl area must remain aware of the uncovered flat and be prepared to attack it if the ball is thrown there. (Diagram 1-14)

DIAGRAM 1-14

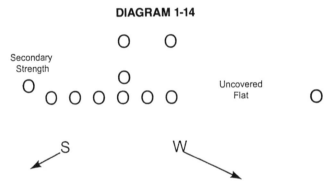

There is a viable solution to eliminating the weakside flat problem. The coverage is called "Money," and it blends very nicely with Green coverage. To the strong side of the formation, the assignments of the C, SS, Sam, and Mike are the same as Green. The FS cheats to the strong side and plays to the strong side of his deep middle one-third zone. To the weak side, the C has #1 in Man-to-Man coverage and the Will has number #2 Man-to-Man. (Diagram 1-15) This protects the weakside flat and is a good change of pace when Green is being used quite a bit in a game. Money is good only if the C and OLB to the weak side are capable of playing Man-to-Man with no additional pressure on the quarterback. Money coverage is employed against all offenses but can be particularly effective against the Wing-T, especially when the Umbrella Look presnap disguise is being employed.

The Mike is responsible for the hook area and normally opens to the side of the tight end on pass recognition. Versus the Wing-T, and any other

DIAGRAM 1-15

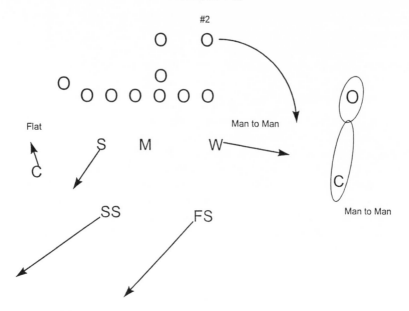

misdirection offense, the Mike *must* be made aware of all crossing patterns. (Diagram 1-16)

Versus the Waggle, Money can cause a defensive problem. The weakside C takes #1 Man-to-Man, and the Will should pick up the fullback (#2) as the fullback attacks the flat area. However, the tight end, running a 12- to 15-yard-deep crossing pattern, could become open in back of the Will and in front of the FS. (Diagram 1-17) For this reason, Money is not

DIAGRAM 1-16

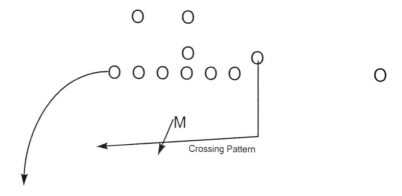

DIAGRAM 1-17

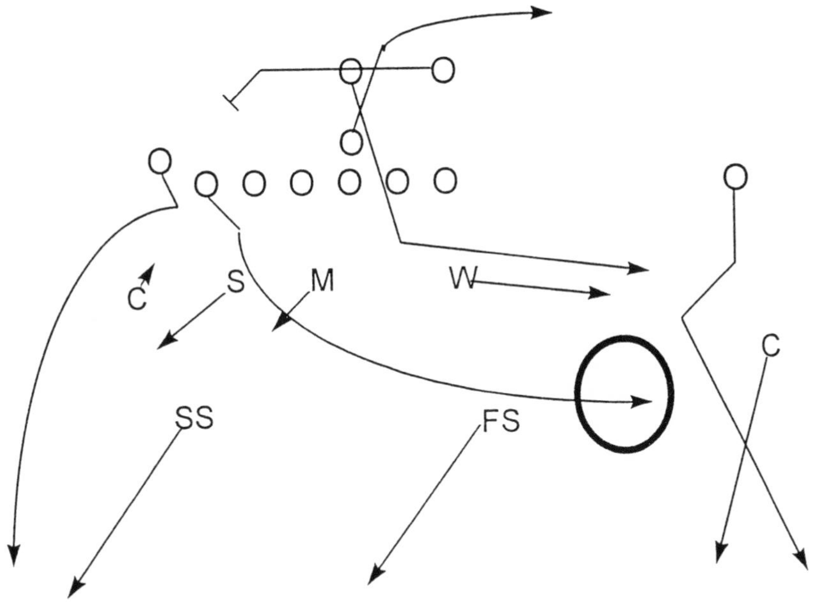

employed at a time when, according to scouting reports, the Waggle is an expected play.

Linebacker Keys

A discussion of linebacker play in our 4–3 defensive package must include an explanation of the linebacker keys. The linebackers read a back and then the "Spot." Versus the Wing-T, all three linebackers normally read the setback (halfback) as their primary key. However, unless they look to the Spot after their initial read, they will be out of position versus most misdirection plays.

Reading the Spot

The three linebackers, after reading their back as their initial key, immediately check the Spot. This is the *most crucial* aspect of the defense when it comes to recognizing and stopping any misdirection run or pass play. The Spot is an imaginary circle directly below the tail of the quarterback when he is under center. When the linebackers see someone (a guard or tackle) cross the Spot in the opposite direction of their backfield key, a misdirection play is being executed. The linebackers adjust their movement and work back toward the ball. This type of key reading takes a great deal of practice and much discipline. With so many offenses making use of the Counter-Gap play and some version of the Waggle, reading the Spot effectively handles these plays. ***Reading the Spot is a "must" in stopping the Wing-T.***

Flopping Defensive Personnel

Because of all the changing of strength prior to the snap of the ball, often employed by the Wing-T and many other offenses, it is advisable not to move defensive personnel with these changes. Both outside linebackers should be capable of playing Will and Sam and both safeties should be able to play Strong and Free. The Wing-T offensive coordinator would prefer to have the defense running around like "Chickens with their heads cut off." Having defenders with the ability to play to the strong side and weak side eliminates this problem.

Chapter 2

4–3 Stunt and Blitz for the Wing-T

The stunt (Split) and blitz (Key Blitz) presented in this chapter are a major part of our 4–3 defensive package. Although they are extremely effective versus the Wing-T, they are equally effective against other offenses. The Split and the Key Blitz are not the only stunt and blitz employed against the Wing-T. However, the Base with Green coverage, Split with Orange Spy coverage, and Key Blitz with He-Man coverage make up 75 percent of the defensive package we employ versus the Wing-T. It is important to remember that much of the effectiveness of these three defenses is predicated on disguise and on not allowing the offense any key as to which defense is about to be executed.

SPLIT

Split, like the Key Blitz, can be executed from a normal Base alignment, the Head-Up alignment or any combination of both. The Head-Up alignment is only effective if, at times, the Base is executed from this alignment. If not, the offense will know that when the Head-Up alignment is used they can expect some type of stunt or blitz.

The Split allows a penetrating gap charge by the four down linemen and one linebacker. At times, penetration can disrupt the Wing-T, especially when the offensive linemen are split a bit too wide or are too slow to protect the offensive gaps. The one problem with a gap charge is the strong possibility of a defensive lineman getting trapped. The Split eliminates or minimizes the possibility of this occurring. Defending against the Trap play is covered in depth later in this book.

The gap-charge technique used by the defensive lineman is very important. The lineman steps with the foot opposite the gap he is attacking (crossover) and aims at a point beyond the gap side leg of the defender on whom he is aligned. He "Rips" with the arm opposite the gap he is attacking and cannot allow the offensive lineman, on whom he is aligned, to prevent him from getting to that gap. Although it is a gap charge, the defensive lineman is under control and does not allow himself to get too much depth before finding the ball. When he is attacked by a trapping offensive lineman, he attempts to react in the same manner as Base. He "Wrong Shoulders" the trapper and forces the back to "Spill" to the outside. If he allows himself too much depth, he cannot handle the trapper in this manner.

The Split, unlike Base, becomes an eight-man-front defense, rather than a seven. This is accomplished by using Orange Spy coverage (Man-to-Man with a free safety) and permitting either the FS or SS to become a pseudo-linebacker, allowing the Will to blitz and have no pass responsibility. Also, unlike Base, the Split allows the Mike to cover only one gap. He is responsible for the strongside A gap and has no responsibility for the weakside B gap. However, like Base, the Mike is expected to read the Spot after he reads the setback as his primary key. Also, unlike Base, Sam employs Man-to-Man coverage on the tight end.

Front Assignments

Remember, the Split can be executed from the Base or Head-Up alignment.

- Strongside End (E) — Gap charge the strongside D gap.
- Strongside Tackle (T) — Gap charge the strongside B gap.
- Weakside Tackle (T) — Gap charge the weakside A gap.
- Weakside End (E) — Gap charge the weakside B gap.
- Strongside Linebacker (Sam) — Strongside C gap, #2 Man-to-Man.
- Middle Linebacker (Mike) — Strongside A gap, #3 Man-to-Man to either side.
- Weakside Linebacker (Will) — Blitz the C gap.

(Diagrams 2-1, Base, and 2-2, Head-Up)

DIAGRAM 2-1

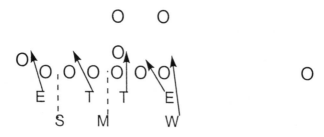

DIAGRAM 2-2

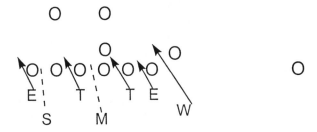

ORANGE SPY

Orange Spy coverage is a form of Man-to-Man coverage with a Free Safety. Unlike normal Man-Free coverage, Sam is responsible for #2 to the tight-end side (strongside for the front), and the SS or FS is responsible for #2 away from the tight end side (weak side for the front). Versus the wing set, the Sam has the tight end (#2) Man-to-Man, while the C has #1 Man-to-Man. These two defenders play an "Inside-Outside" rule in this situation. Sam covers either receiver who becomes the inside receiver and the C covers either receiver who becomes the outside receiver. If the wing runs an inside pattern and the tight end goes outside, the Sam picks up the wing and the tight end is covered by the C.

DIAGRAM 2-3

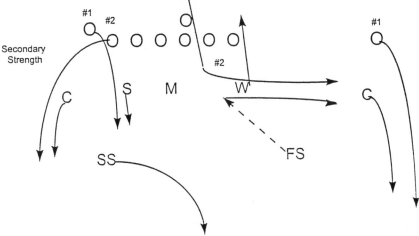

Since the FS is aligned away from the tight end and the direction of the Split (secondary strength declared to the tight-end side), he is responsible for weak #2 and, prior to the snap of the ball, he begins to cheat up to be more effective in the running game. (Diagram 2-3)

Versus the slot set, the Sam has #2 and the C has the tight end (#1). The Inside-Outside rule remains in effect. Since the SS is aligned away from the tight end (and the direction of the Split), he is responsible for covering the slot (#2) Man-to-Man. Like the FS, prior to the snap of the ball, he cheats up to be more effective in the running game. (Diagram 2-4)

DIAGRAM 2-4

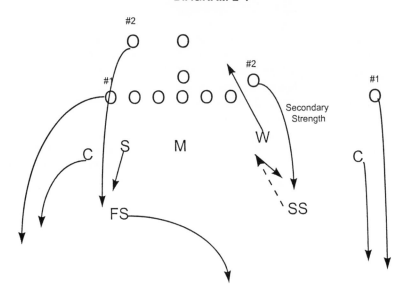

Secondary Assignments

- Corners — #1 Man-to-Man
- SS or FS — #2 Away from the tight end
- SS or FS — Free (deep middle one-third zone)

KEY BLITZ

Key Blitz involves a blitz by one, two, or three linebackers, a gap charge by one defensive lineman and a slant charge by the other three defensive linemen. Unlike Split, Key Blitz remains a seven-man front but provides five or six defenders to attack the pass, with the possibility of seven versus the Waggle play.

Key Blitz is excellent against the run because it allows the linebackers to blitz gaps according to a key rather than in a predetermined gap. For this reason, the Key Blitz is referred to as a "Flow" blitz. All three linebackers, as in Base, key the setback (halfback) as their primary key. However, only the outside linebacker away from the flow of the key reads the Spot while the other two blitz.

When the key steps toward the strong side, the Sam blitzes the D gap and the Mike blitzes the B gap. The Will executes a "Hitman technique" by very slowly flowing toward the play side and looking for a cutback while reading the Spot. If the Waggle develops to the weak side, the Will immediately attacks the quarterback.

When the key steps toward the weak side, the Will blitzes the C gap and the Mike quickly flows to the play side, but does not blitz. The Sam executes the Hitman technique and reacts in the same manner as the Will when flow went to the strong side.

Versus the slot formation, there is a modification when flow goes to the side of the slot (the weak side). The Will blitzes the D gap, and the Mike blitzes the B gap. The Sam executes his Hitman technique.

The slant charge by the defensive lineman, like the gap charge, is very important. The lineman aims at a point directly below the helmet of the offensive lineman to whom he is slanting. He either crossover steps or directly steps to that "Target Point." He gets a piece of that offensive player if possible. If the offensive lineman vacates the area and the defensive lineman cannot get a piece of him, the defensive lineman does not penetrate. He attempts to locate and attack the ball. If an offensive blocker attempts to trap him, he plays it in the same manner as the gap charge.

Front Assignments

- Strongside End (E) — Slant to the near ear of the offensive tackle (C-gap responsibility).
- Strongside Tackle (T) — Slant to the near ear of the center (A-gap responsibility).
- Weakside Tackle (T) — Gap charge the weakside A gap (A-gap responsibility).
- Weakside End (E) — Versus an open end, slant to the near eye of the offensive guard (B-gap responsibility). Versus a slot, slant to the near eye of the slot (C-gap responsibility).
- Strongside Linebacker (Sam) — Strongside flow, blitz the D gap. Weakside flow, Hitman technique.

- Middle Linebacker (Mike) — Strongside flow, blitz the strongside B gap. Weakside flow, flow weakside. Versus a slot, blitz the weakside B gap.
- Weakside Linebacker (Will) — Strongside flow, Hitman technique. Weakside flow, blitz C gap. Versus a slot, blitz the weakside D gap.

(Diagrams 2-5, 2-6, and 2-7)

DIAGRAM 2-5

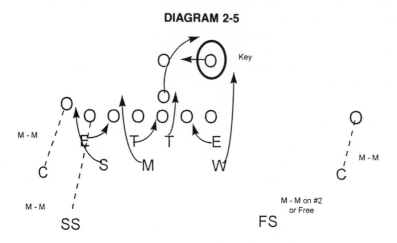

DIAGRAM 2-6

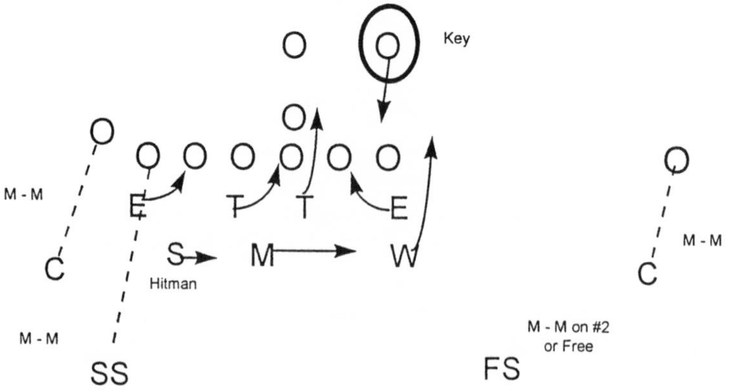

DIAGRAM 2-7

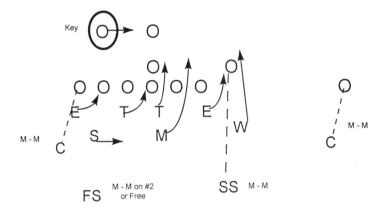

HE-MAN

He-Man is pure Man coverage with the possibility of having a Free Safety. Normal Man coverage rules apply, with each C being responsible for #1 to his side. The SS covers #2 to the strong side. In this coverage, the secondary always declares the wing/tight-end side of the formation as the strong side. The FS is responsible for #2 to the weak side. If no #2 releases to the weak side, the FS becomes free and covers the deep middle area. Since there is, at least, one linebacker executing a blitz (and the strong possibility of two or three), Man coverage can be effective because of strong pressure being exerted on the quarterback. Both the blitzing and the Hitman outside linebackers are responsible for #3 to their side. The blitzing linebacker employs a "Blitz Peel" technique. This coverage is excellent as long as the slanting linemen tie up offensive blockers and the gap-charging tackle and the blitzing linebacker(s) get to the quarterback.

Both Split and Key Blitz are potent in most down-and-distance situations and work very well versus the running game and play-action passing game. They can be effective in a long-yardage situation, but normally Base, with some type of blitz, or a Nickel type of defense is used in this situation.

SOME THOUGHTS PRIOR TO DEFENDING VARIOUS WING-T PLAYS

With everything being equal, the Wing-T Offense, or any offense, should be effective against a defense that remains unchanged throughout an entire game. For the offensive personnel to know where the defenders will align and how they will react to different plays is a tremendous advantage for the offense and the offensive coordinator.

When the 4–3 Defense, or any defense based on solid fundamentals, faces any offense, it behooves the defensive coordinator to have enough variations in his defensive package to cause confusion for the offensive players. Rarely, if ever, will a defensive coordinator allow his players to sit in one defense for an entire game, unless his personnel are greatly superior to the offensive personnel they are facing. Disguise and variation are great equalizers for any defensive unit.

In the following chapters of this book, the 4–3 Defense is pitted against the dynamic Wing-T Offense. However, the defense may present only one or two initial looks and execute three different defenses from those looks. For example, the strongside offensive guard will see the defensive tackle align in two different alignments (2 technique and 3 technique) and execute three different assignments (Read, Gap, and Slant). The quarterback and receivers will see a secondary in an initial Umbrella Look, then carry out three different coverage schemes (Green, Orange Spy, and He-Man).

The 4–3 defensive package presented here consists of a very solid Base defense and two excellent variations. By using all three, and not giving any key to which one is being employed, the entire package can and will be extremely effective.

Remember, to be effective, all three must be done from the Base and Head-Up look, unless all three are effectively executed from just one of those alignments.

Chapter 3

Defending the Sweep and Trap

SWEEP

The Sweep is one of the prime plays employed by the Wing-T to attack the flank. The mechanics of the Sweep are unique, as they present the defense with the threat of being attacked in three possible areas. The play threatens both D gaps and the playside A gap. The Sweep itself attacks the playside D gap. The Waggle threatens the offside D gap, and also menaces the secondary with the possibility of a pass; the Trap threatens the playside A gap. To properly defend the Sweep, the other two possible plays must also be considered.

Base 4–3 with Green Coverage

In a definite running down situation, the secondary would declare strength to the wing/tight-end side of the formation. This could present problems if the offense runs the Waggle. (The Waggle play is discussed in Chapter 6.)

The strongside E (playside E) attacks the tight end and makes sure he gets a piece of him to prevent the tight end from getting a clean shot at Sam or Mike. As the tight end releases inside, the E steps with his outside foot, making his shoulders nearly perpendicular to the LOS. The E looks inside for a pulling guard or the fullback attempting to kick him out. The E intends to wrong shoulder any kickout block while still being aware of the possibility of a down block by the wing. Normally, being a bigger and stronger athlete than the wing, the E may be blocked to the inside by the wing but should not be collapsed. Due to his perpendicular position on the LOS and his strength and size advantage, the E should see the depth of the pulling guards and be able to attack one of them. He may not be able to get the playside guard but, hopefully, will be able to get a piece of the offside guard and knock him off-track as he attempts to attack the ballcarrier.

The strongside T (playside T) attacks the offensive guard and immediately reads the guard's outside pull. Fearing a false pull by the guard to set up the trap by the offside guard, the T closes to the inside to wrong shoulder the trap. In this position, the T is vulnerable to a down block by the playside tackle. The T could be collapsed, but it is worthwhile for this to occur in order for the T to be in a good position to stop the Trap play. Once he feels the down block by the tackle, he fights through the pressure and attempts to get into the correct pursuit angle to get into the play. If the T is quick enough to avoid the down block of the tackle (this is not likely) and make the play, the next offensive play may be the Trap. This is one way the Wing-T handles a 3 technique who is overly aggressive and capable of stopping the Sweep. (Diagram 3-1)

The weakside T (offside T) attacks the center and is blocked by the center. The T fights through the pressure, like the 3 technique, and gets into the correct pursuit angle to get into the play.

The weakside E (offside E) attacks the tackle and reads the tackle's attempt to cut him off from the play. Once the E recognizes that the play is being run away from him, it is his responsibility to trail the play and look for any Counter or Reverse.

The Sam (playside OLB) reads his key (the setback) and sees the key step toward the strong side. The Sam takes a parallel step to the outside and immediately looks to the Spot. When he sees the offside guard cross the Spot in the same direction as the key, he feels the ball is coming to the strong side. His slight outside step, along with the attack of the 7 technique, prohibits the tight end from blocking him and allows the tight end to go inside to block the Mike. The Sam is now the target of the offside pulling guard who attempts to pull through the hole and cut off the Sam. The Sam steps up to the hole (D gap) and attacks the offside guard; he is, hopefully, in great position to make the play. (Diagram 3-2)

The Mike reads his key and sees the key step toward the strong side. Since Mike is a "downhill" player, he steps up toward the strongside A gap, his area of responsibility versus a running play to the strong side. He reads the Spot and sees the offside guard cross it. He realizes the play is going to

DIAGRAM 3-1

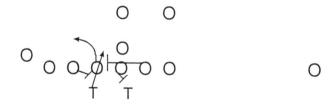

DIAGRAM 3-2

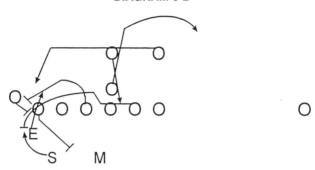

the strong side. The tight end, after being attacked by the 7 technique, has a clear shot at the Mike. Once the Mike recognizes Sweep, he attacks the tight end and fights through the tight end's face to get to the play. The Mike is expected to get into the correct pursuit angle and get in on the play.

The Will (offside OLB) reads his key (the setback) and sees the key step toward the strong side. The Sam takes a parallel step to the play side and looks to the Spot. When he sees the offside guard cross the Spot, he assumes the Hitman technique but, since no offensive player crossed the Spot in the direction opposite the key, he does not expect Waggle or a Counter. However, he slowly flows playside, looking for a cutback. Once the threat of cutback disappears, the Will gets into the proper pursuit angle.

With strength declared to the wing/tight-end side, the C (playside C) reads the handoff by the quarterback and sees the wing block down on the 7 technique. He recognizes the running play and, due to the tight split of #1, is the secondary player responsible to force the run. Once the threat of a play-action pass is gone, the C comes up to a point on the LOS where the wing originally aligned. (Diagram 3-3) If he comes up too wide, the playside

DIAGRAM 3-3

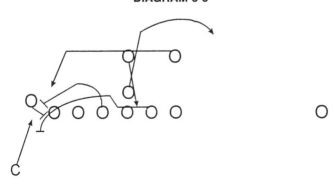

pulling guard will have an angle from which to kick out the C. He stays on the LOS and avoids the block of the playside guard. The C and the Sam are the two defenders expected to stop the play at the point of attack.

The SS (playside S) begins rotating to the deep outside one-third zone. When he recognizes run and all threat of a pass is gone, he attacks the play from the outside-in. He cannot come up until the ballcarrier crosses the LOS. He must protect against an HB pass before he commits to the running play.

The FS (offside S), upon recognition of run and no threat of a pass, becomes the "Alley Player" and slowly attacks the play from the inside-out. He looks for any cutback while flowing to the ball.

The C (offside C), when the threat of a pass is gone, carefully rotates through the deep middle zone, looking for any cutback. He provides the last line of defense against the run and is expected to make the tackle only if the ballcarrier breaks free of the other defenders. (Diagram 3-4)

When the secondary declares strength to the split-end side, rather than the wing/tight-end side, the secondary run support to the play side is much slower. This can cause a real problem in stopping the Sweep. The playside C covers the playside deep outside one-third zone before forcing the run. This provides the offense with a "Soft Corner" and the possibility of a big play. This problem is one reason for the Split and the Key Blitz and why

DIAGRAM 3-4

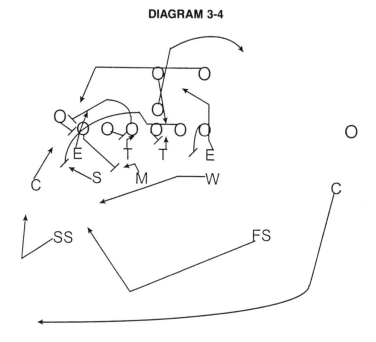

DIAGRAM 3-5

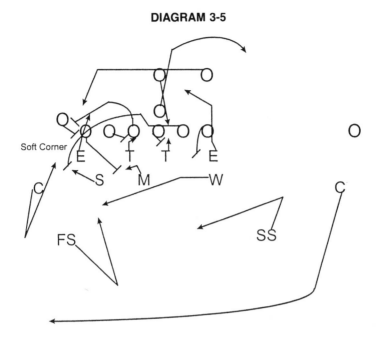

coverages other than Green are often employed versus the Wing-T Offense.
(Diagram 3-5)

Split with Orange Spy Coverage

The strongside E (playside E) executes a gap charge through the
playside D gap. He meets the wing, attempting to down block on the E.
Being bigger and stronger than the wing, he forces, at least, a stalemate at
the point of attack. This deadlock causes a wider flank than the offense
faced when executing the Sweep versus the Base 4–3, resulting in possible
confusion for the playside pulling guard as to which defensive player he
should attempt to block. This charge by the E, in itself, can be the main
ingredient in stopping the play. Unfortunately, with the gap charge by the E,
the tight end is left untouched and has an unimpeded path to the Sam.

The strongside T (playside T) attacks the playside B gap with a gap
charge. Like the E meeting the wing, the T meets the tackle attempting to
down block on him. Since the E does not normally have a strength or size
advantage over the tackle, a stalemate is an acceptable result of this
collision. However, the T cannot allow himself to be driven toward the offside
or off the ball. The T fights through the face of the tackle, attempting to fill
the C gap with the tackle. The T does not cross the face of the tackle but

DIAGRAM 3-6

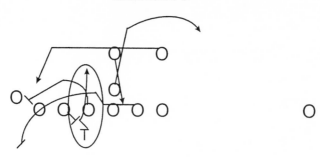

rather pushes the tackle into the hole. If the T can go around the block of the tackle (into the backfield) and make the play, he is allowed to use this "Backdoor Move." (Diagram 3-6) However, he must make the play or he has taken himself totally out of any good pursuit angle.

The weakside T (offside T) gap charges the offside A gap. Unlike the other gap-charging defensive linemen, the offside T is encouraged to be a bit more reckless and to get more depth into the backfield before finding the ball. There is little chance a Wing-T team will attempt to trap a 1 technique. They are much more likely to attempt a trap on the 3 technique.

If the T is quick enough to beat the block of the center, he runs into the fullback as the fullback attempts to block him. The fullback's main job is to eliminate penetration through the A gap. If the center does get a piece of the T and pushes him to the offside, the T continues upfield to force the fullback to block him. The T has to occupy the fullback to give the offside E a chance to make a big play.

The weakside E (offside E) gap charges through the offside B gap. The offensive tackle attempts to cut off the E and prevent penetration. The E, as he is executing a good gap charge technique by making sure his outside arm and leg go across the face of the offside tackle, sees the pull of the offside guard. Since the E is careful not to get too much depth into the backfield, he should avoid the collision of the offside T and fullback. As the E follows the pull of the offside guard, he locates the ball and should make the tackle before the ballcarrier reaches the LOS. The offside E is the defender who often stops this play. However, it is critical for him to beat the block of the offside tackle. If it is necessary for the E to align in a 4 technique to effectively execute his gap charge, he *must* employ the Head-Up alignment. (Diagram 3-7)

The Sam (playside OLB) has the tight end Man-to-Man. The E keys the tight end all the way and does not key the setback or the Spot. Since the tight end is not touched by the playside E, he has a clear shot at the Sam. Since the Sam is keying the tight end, the Sam immediately sees the tight

DIAGRAM 3-7

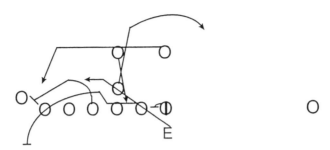

end's attempted block and attacks the tight end trying to jam the tight end into the D gap.

The Mike, seeing his key step to the strong side, takes a step up to the playside A gap. The offside pulling guard, crossing the Spot, assures the Mike the play is going to the strong side. After locating the ball, Mike flows toward the play. However, the Mike must avoid the pile created by the tight end blocking the Sam.

The Will (offside OLB) executes his blitz into the C gap. He may carry out this blitz from his 50 technique or he may move to the LOS, prior to the snap, and blitz from there. As he blitzes into the backfield, he sees his key step away from him. He looks immediately to the quarterback for Waggle. Once the threat of Waggle has passed, the Will assumes the job of the offside E in the Base 4–3. The Will trails the play and looks for any Counter or Reverse.

The strongside C (playside C) playing the wing Man-to-Man, sees the wing make contact with the E. The C waits to be sure the wing is truly blocking and not attempting a late pass release. When the threat of pass is gone, the C attacks the LOS in the same manner that he attacked the LOS when employing Green coverage.

The SS (playside safety), on the snap of the ball, begins to drop as he becomes free and is responsible for the deep middle area. When the SS recognizes a running play and knows that the threat of a passing play is gone, he becomes the Alley Player and attacks the play from the inside-out.

The FS (offside S), prior to the snap, cheats up toward the LOS and takes his place as a pseudo-linebacker. He keys the setback and makes sure the fullback does not sneak out as the #2 receiver. Since no #2 releases for a pass, the FS becomes the Hitman and looks for a cutback.

The weakside C (offside C) plays the weakside #1 with Man-to-Man coverage. The C plays inside leverage on #1 until he recognizes run. The main responsibility of the C is Man-to-Man coverage, and he is not expected to get into the running play until very late. (Diagram 3-8)

DIAGRAM 3-8

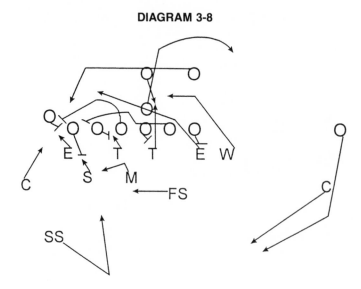

Key Blitz with He-Man Coverage

The strongside E (playside E) slants to the near eye of the tackle. The E crosses the face of the tight end and should be blocked by the tight end to the inside. Since the E is moving in the same direction as the direction of the block, the E is taken away from the point of attack. Since the tackle is blocking to the inside, there is a possibility the E could attack the running back through the area vacated by the tackle.

The strongside T (playside T) slants to the near eye of the center. The tackle steps to block the T to the inside. With the T already moving to the inside, contact between the tackle and the T is slightly delayed. This delay, along with the center blocking to the offside, forces the T to consider the possibility of a trap by the offside pulling guard. The T turns his shoulders perpendicular to the LOS in an attempt to wrong shoulder the trap if it appears. Seeing no trap, and being somewhat distant from the tackle moving to block the T to the inside, the T might be able to leak into the backfield and, possibly, make a play. This could happen but normally does not. When the T feels the block of the tackle, he tries to fight through the block and get back into the play.

Neither the strongside E nor the T is expected to make the play on the Sweep. If one of them does make the play, it is a real bonus.

The weakside T (offside T) does exactly the same thing in Key Blitz that he does in Split.

The weakside E (offside E) slants to the near eye of the offensive guard. Just as in Split, the E beats the block of the offside tackle and he may have to align in a 4 technique to accomplish this goal. The E follows the pull of the offside guard and, since the E is slanting, he does not have to worry about getting too much depth. He locates the ball and is in great position to stop the ballcarrier before the back reaches the LOS. As in Split, the E is often the defender who stops the Sweep.

The Sam (playside OLB) reads his key and sees the setback move toward the strong side. The Sam blitzes the playside D gap where he meets the attempted block by the wing. Like the E in Split, the Sam should be bigger and stronger than the wing and should force, at least, a stalemate at the point of attack. This stalemate often forces the playside pulling guard to adjust his path and go wider than the guard would like. The Sam fights through the face of the wing and forces the flank to widen.

The Mike, reading his key, blitzes the playside B gap. With the tight end blocking the E and the tackle blocking the T, a natural hole opens up, allowing the Mike entry into the backfield through the B gap. Often the Mike stops the Sweep for a loss. (Diagram 3-9)

The Will (offside OLB), with his key going to the strong side and no offensive player crossing the Spot opposite the direction of the key, becomes the Hitman. He looks for cutback and gets in the proper pursuit angle to meet the Sweep if the setback crosses the LOS.

The strongside C (playside C) and the weakside C do exactly the same thing in He-Man coverage that they did in Orange Spy.

The SS (playside safety) reads the block of the tight end. When the SS is sure the threat of a play-action pass is gone, he attacks the sweep from the inside-out and attacks the offside pulling guard.

DIAGRAM 3-9

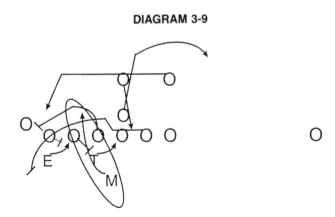

DIAGRAM 3-10

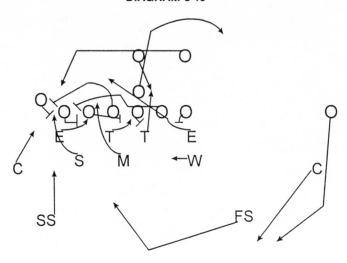

The FS (offside safety) makes sure there is no #2 releasing for a pass to the weak side. He then begins to drop toward the deep middle. When he recognizes run, he becomes the Alley Player and carefully attacks the play from the inside-out. (Diagram 3-10)

TRAP

The Fullback Trap is the middle attacking play in the Sweep series. Versus the 4–3 Defense, the intention of the offense is to trap the 3 technique. When the offensive coordinator knows the 3 technique is overpenetrating and causing trouble for the Sweep, the Fullback Trap is the solution to this problem.

Although the Trap can be executed with several different blocking schemes to the play side, in this description the inside release by the playside guard, rather than the false outside pull, is used. Furthermore, the three linebackers (when it applies) read their key (the setback) and the Spot and get the same initial reads as the Sweep. To eliminate unnecessary duplication, the description of the linebackers' reactions to the Trap take place after their initial reads.

Base 4–3 with Green Coverage

Like the Sweep, in a definite running down situation, the secondary declares strength to the wing/tight-end side of the formation.

The strongside E (playside E) attacks the tight end, and the tight end attempts to turn the E out. The E fights through the face of the tight end and forces the tight end into the C gap. The E is in a position to make the play when the defensive T forces the ballcarrier to spill to the outside.

The strongside T (playside T) attacks the playside guard as the guard releases to the inside to block the Mike. The T gets a piece of the guard to prevent the guard from getting a clean shot at the Mike. As the guard releases to the inside, the T steps with his outside foot, making his shoulders nearly perpendicular to the LOS. The T immediately looks for the trapping offside guard. The T attacks the trapper and wrong shoulders the blocker. The T does not wait for the trapper. He *attacks* the trapper! The attack by the T, with his backfield-side shoulder, prevents the trap block and leaves no hole for the fullback. The fullback is forced to spill to the outside. The play of the T is the most important aspect of stopping the play. The T *must* wrong shoulder the trapper! (Diagram 3-11)

The weakside T (offside T) attacks the center as the center attempts to block him. The T does not give any ground and fights through the face of the center, jamming the center into the playside A gap. Forcing the center into the playside A gap, along with the Wrong Shoulder by the playside T, severely restricts the size of the playside A and B gaps. The offside T may not make the tackle but his job of forcing the center into the A gap is every bit as important as making the tackle.

The weakside E (offside E) attacks the tackle and reads the tackle's attempt to cut him off. The E forces the tackle into the offside B gap and fights through the tackle's face to the ball upon recognition of the play.

The Sam (playside OLB) fights through the attempted cutoff block by the playside tackle. Although his keys indicated Sweep, the block by the tackle tells him otherwise. The Sam fights through the face of the tackle, forcing the tackle into the playside B gap. The Sam and the playside E are in a great position to make the play on the fullback as he spills to the outside.

DIAGRAM 3-11

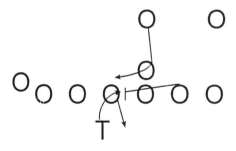

DIAGRAM 3-12

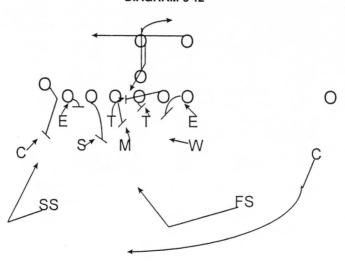

The Mike steps up toward the A gap and sees the playside guard attempting to block him. The contact on the playside guard by the playside T determines how much time the Mike has to react to the attempted block by the guard. The Mike attacks the guard and fights through his face as he pushes the guard into the B gap. The Mike cannot allow himself to be blocked back or toward the offside. By pushing the guard into the B gap, the Mike, along with the play of the playside T and the offside T, clogs the hole where the fullback intends to run.

The Will, as the Hitman, begins his slow flow toward the play side. The Will checks for Waggle before he moves from his initial alignment. If the fullback, seeing the trap hole closed, decides to cut back to the offside of the center, the Will's job is to be in position to stop him.

The secondary, too, rotates in the same manner that it did versus the Sweep. Both the safeties, upon recognition of the inside running play, attack the play from the inside-out. (Diagram 3-12)

Split with Orange Spy Coverage

The Split is not the best defense to employ against the Trap. However, with good play by the offside T, the offside E, and the FS, the play can be stopped in its tracks.

The strongside E (playside E) gap charges through the strongside D gap. He actually takes himself out of the play and can get involved only if the fullback breaks the LOS and the E makes a play while pursuing the ballcarrier.

The strongside T (playside T) executes his gap charge through the strongside B gap. His gap charge actually opens up the B gap and creates a natural running lane for the fullback. When the T sees and feels the playside tackle bypass him and go to the next level, the T realizes he is going to be trapped. The T turns to the inside and must force the offside pulling guard to block him and not turn up into the hole. Depending on how the offside pulling guard is coached, the guard may ignore the T and turn up into the hole to pick up another defender because he feels the T is too wide and not able to make the play. The T must do everything in his power to force the guard to block him, or the guard could pick off the FS as the FS flows to make the play. (Diagram 3-13)

The weakside T (offside T) charges through the offside A gap. If the T is quick enough and makes use of the totally correct gap-charge technique, he will either beat the block of the center or force the center to only get a piece of him. The T often makes the play on the fullback or collides with the offside pulling guard and knocks the guard off his Trap path.

The weakside E (offside E) charges through the offside B gap. If the E beats the block of the offside T, as he is expected to do, and does not allow himself too much depth into the backfield, he ends up in the fullback's face and tackles the back for a loss. This is another situation where aligning in the 4 technique really helps the charge of the E.

The Sam (playside OLB), keying the tight end, sees him take an outside step to block the playside E. The Sam has to be sure the tight end is blocking before he can turn his attention to the inside to find the ball. When the Sam realizes it is the Trap, he has the playside offensive tackle in his face. He fights through the face of the tackle, attempting to jam the tackle into the B gap. The Sam is in excellent position to make the play if the playside T forces the fullback to spill to the outside.

The Mike takes a step up into the playside A gap, knowing the playside guard is untouched and has a clear shot at him. As in the Base 4–3, the Mike attacks the guard and pushes him into the B gap. The push of the

DIAGRAM 3-13

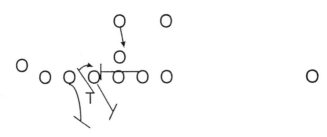

guard by the Mike is important in the Base 4–3 but *crucial* in the Split. The gap-charging playside T creates a natural hole for the fullback, and the Mike must do his part to restrict the hole. When the offside T or E does not make the play (very rare), the Mike is put in the situation of having to make an excellent play.

The Will (offside OLB) blitzes the offside C gap. The main responsibility of the Will is to stop the Waggle. If he locates the ball soon enough, he may be a factor in stopping the Trap, but normally the Will is not involved with stopping the play.

The playside C and the offside C are in Man-to-Man coverage and are not expected to get into the running play until very late.

The SS (playside safety) begins his deep middle drop and cannot commit to the LOS until he is sure the threat of a pass is gone. The SS becomes the last line of defense to stop the fullback if he breaks through the LOS.

The FS (offside safety), assuming his role as a linebacker, is unaccounted for in the blocking scheme and is the defender who makes the play if the fullback makes it to the LOS. This is where Orange Spy coverage really pays dividends. (Diagram 3-14)

Key Blitz with He-Man Coverage

The strongside E (playside E) slants to the near eye of the tackle. The tight end, stepping to the inside in an attempt to cut off the E, may get a piece of the E but cannot prevent the E from getting inside. The E, seeing

DIAGRAM 3-14

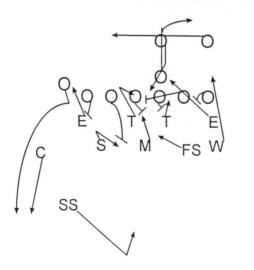
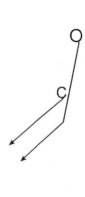

the tackle release from the LOS to cut off the Sam, recognizes the trap-blocking scheme and continues along the LOS to the inside. The E turns to the inside and attacks the trapper with the Wrong Shoulder. The E has good inside momentum and makes excellent contact with the offside trapping guard, forcing the fullback to spill to the outside.

The strongside T (playside T) slants to the near eye of the center. The playside guard, having the T cross his face, may step to block the T to the inside or the guard may bypass the T and go to the next level. If the guard bypasses the T to go to the next level to block the Mike, the T, seeing the center block to the offside, attacks the offside trapping guard. This scenario causes the trapper to make his block prematurely and totally clogs the hole for the fullback, forcing the fullback to spill to the outside or attempt to cut back. (Diagram 3-15)

The weakside T (offside T) does exactly the same thing in Key Blitz that he does in Split.

The weakside E (offside E) slants to the near eye of the offensive guard. Just as in Split, the E beats the block of the offside tackle. The E may have to align in a 4 technique to accomplish this goal. The E follows the pull of the offside guard and, since the E is slanting and not employing a gap charge, he is operating along the LOS and not getting depth into the backfield. He locates the ball and is in a great position to collide with the fullback. As in Split, the E is often the defender who stops the Trap.

The Sam (onside OLB) blitzes the playside D gap and is out of position to make a tackle on the Trap. When the tight end cannot get a piece of the E, he often continues to the next level and attempts to keep the Sam to the outside.

The Mike, blitzing the playside B gap, meets the tackle and, fighting through his face, forces the tackle into the B gap. Since the Mike is blitzing to the B gap, he has momentum and can get no less than a stalemate with the tackle. The Mike cannot allow himself to be moved to the inside.

The Will, being the Hitman, checks for Waggle before flowing toward

DIAGRAM 3-15

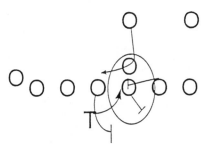

DIAGRAM 3-16

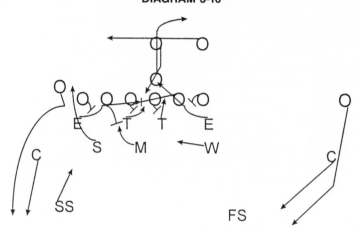

the play. If the fullback is not spilled to the outside (play side), the Will often makes the play.

The playside C and the offside C are in Man-to-Man coverage and are not expected to get into the running play until very late.

The SS (playside safety) reads the block of the tight end. When the SS is sure the threat of a play-action pass is gone, he recognizes the running play and comes up to make the play. The SS often makes the play when the fullback spills to the outside.

The FS (offside safety) makes sure there is no #2 releasing for a pass to the weak side. He then begins to drop toward the deep middle. When he recognizes Trap, the FS approaches the LOS and carefully attacks the play, as he is the last defender between the LOS and the goal line. (Diagram 3-16)

KEY POINTS TO STOPPING THE SWEEP

Base

1. The playside E must get a good piece of the tight end to prevent the tight end from getting a free shot at the Sam.

2. The playside E cannot allow himself to be collapsed by the block of the wing.

3. The playside C must replace the wing when the C comes up to stop the play. The C cannot come up too wide.

Split

1. On his gap charge, the playside E must push the wing out and force the flank to widen.

2. The offside E cannot get blocked by the offside tackle.

3. The playside C must react quickly to run.

Key Blitz

1. The blitzing Sam must force the wing outside and make the flank widen.

2. The Mike must get through the hole developing in the B gap.

3. The playside C must react quickly to run.

KEY POINTS TO STOPPING THE TRAP

Base

1. The playside T must wrong shoulder the trapper.

2. The offside T must jam the center into the playside A gap.

3. The Mike must force the playside guard into the playside B gap.

Split

1. The playside T must force the trapper to block him.

2. The offside E must avoid the block of the offside tackle.

3. The FS has to get involved in the play.

Key Blitz

1. The playside E must recognize the trap-blocking scheme and wrong shoulder the trapper.

2. The Mike must fight through the face of the playside tackle and force the tackle into the B gap.

Chapter 4

Defending the Belly and HB Counter

BELLY

Like the Sweep, the Belly action presents the defense with the possibility of multiple plays. Versus the 4–3 Defense, the Belly attacks the weakside B gap. The Belly Option and the Belly Pass are two possible plays coming off the Belly action to the weak side. The HB Counter comes off the Belly action but the point of attack is the strong side of the formation.

The Wing-T employs various blocking schemes when executing the Belly to the weak side. "On," "Cross," and "Wham" are the three most common variations. The On blocking scheme is used in this discussion. Motion by the wing is also included in this chapter.

Base 4–3 with Green Coverage

Again, in a definite running down situation, the secondary normally declares strength to the wing/tight-end side. However, wing motion could make the secondary change the strength call to the direction of the motion. In this scenario, the FS becomes the SS and is responsible for the curl-to-flat coverage, due to the wide split of #1, and the SS becomes the FS. In this chapter, the secondary changes the strength call with the wing motion. (Diagram 4-1)

The strongside E (offside E) attacks the tight end as the tight end attempts to cut off the E. The E, seeing the play being run to the original weak side, gets as deep as the deepest back and trails the play looking for Counter or Reverse.

The strongside T (offside T) attacks the strongside guard and reads the guard's weakside pull. The T expects a block by the center and attacks the center as the center steps to him. The T fights through the face of the center, forcing the center into the playside A gap. The T does not cross the

DIAGRAM 4-1

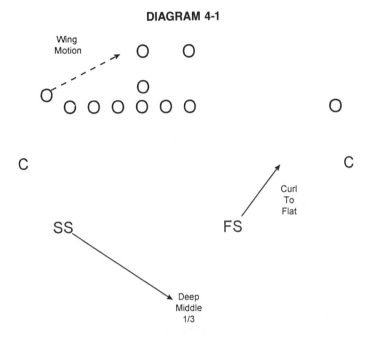

face of the center, as this would open the offside A gap for cutback. (Diagram 4-2)

The weakside T (playside T) attacks the center and feels the center stepping to the offside. Being a 1 technique, the T does not expect to be trapped by the weakside guard, but does expect a down block by the playside guard. The T steps to the playside guard and attacks him, fighting through the guard's face and forcing the guard into the B gap. The play of the T is crucial to stopping the play. The T cannot allow himself to be moved inside or off the LOS. The T has to get, at least, a stalemate. Preferably, the T

DIAGRAM 4-2

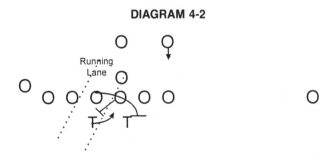

can force the guard back into the play and really constrict the playside B gap.

The weakside E (playside E) attacks the playside tackle and feels the attempted turnout block by the tackle. Like the playside T, the E must force the tackle into the B gap. A stalemate between the E and the tackle is acceptable but certainly not preferred. The more the T and E constrict the B gap, the more effective the Will and Mike will be in stopping the play.

The Sam (offside OLB) sees his key (setback) step to the weak side and sees no offensive player cross the Spot toward the Sam. The Sam knows there is no Counter coming to his side. The S also notices the wing motion, but this has no effect on his initial reads. The Sam becomes the Hitman and avoids any cutoff attempt by the offside tackle as the Sam cautiously flows toward the play.

The Mike reads the setback step to the weak side. The Mike also views the offside guard pull across the Spot in an attempt to cut off the Mike. The Mike avoids the blocking attempt by the pulling offside guard and steps up to his weakside area of responsibility, the B gap. The Mike attacks the setback, from the inside-out, as the setback attempts to block through the B gap.

In the Base 4–3, the Will (playside OLB) is the key defensive player to stop the Belly. The Will's basic rule is to attack the B gap when two offensive backs attempt to go through it. When one offensive back attacks the B gap, the Will is responsible for the D gap. When the Will reads the two backs attacking the B gap, he attacks the play from the outside-in. The Will attacks the play with his inside shoulder and prevents the fullback from breaking to the outside if the setback blocks or shields the Mike from the B gap. If the setback attempts to block the Will instead of the Mike, the Mike should make the play. (Diagram 4-3)

The SS (offside S), on the change of strength, becomes the FS and begins to rotate into the deep middle one-third zone. When he recognizes run, he becomes the Alley Player and slowly attacks the play from the inside-out.

DIAGRAM 4-3

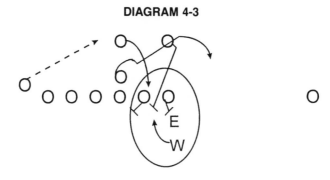

DIAGRAM 4-4

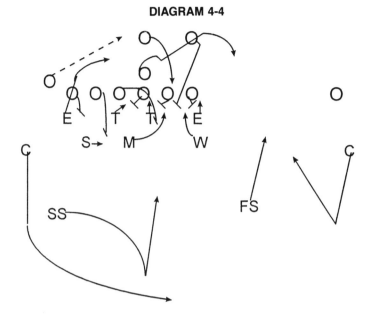

The FS (playside S), on the change of strength, becomes the SS and goes through the curl area to the flat area on the snap of the ball. When the SS reads the Belly, he stays outside in anticipation of Belly Option or Belly Pass. When he sees the setback go through the B gap, the SS believes the chance of a Belly Option or Belly Pass is very slim, and he begins to fall inside toward the B gap.

The C (offside C) drops to the deep outside one-third zone. When he recognizes weakside run, the C carefully rotates through the deep middle zone, looking for cutback.

The C (playside) begins to drop to the deep outside one-third zone. When he recognizes a run, and is sure all threat of a pass is gone, the C attacks the play from the outside-in. (Diagram 4-4)

Split with Orange Spy Coverage

The strongside E (offside E) charges through the strongside D gap. His charge takes him away from the play. When the E realizes the offensive action is going away from him, he checks for Waggle and then trails the play, looking for Counter or Reverse.

The strongside T (offside T) executes his gap charge through the offside B gap. Like the strongside E, the charge of the T takes him away from the play, but the T has a slight chance of falling back into the play. If the T, executing his charge, either sees or feels the playside guard vacate the

DIAGRAM 4-5

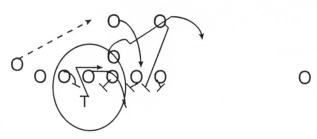

area while pulling to the play side, the T attempts to break back to the play side. The offside tackle steps into the B gap to protect the gap against penetration. The T cannot allow the tackle to get between himself and the ball. The T must keep on the play side of the tackle's attempted cutoff block. (Diagram 4-5)

The weakside T (playside T) gap charges the playside A gap. Although the playside guard has an excellent angle to block the T, it is hoped the T can get some penetration and cause some problems for the play. However, the T cannot be relied upon to make the play.

The weakside E (playside E) attacks the playside B gap. The playside tackle, employing his gap-blocking rule, should attempt to block the gap-charging E to the inside. If the tackle is quick enough to pick up the E, the tackle has a good angle and could pin the E inside. This scheme forces the setback to block outside the block of the tackle. The E must fight against the block of the tackle, and attempt to get into the play. Like the playside T, the E cannot be expected to make the play unless he is quick enough to beat the block of the tackle, and this often occurs because the playside tackle is not expecting an inside gap charge. (Diagram 4-6)

The Sam (offside OLB) no longer has the tight end with Man-to-Man coverage. The wing motion forces the C to cover the tight end with Man-to-Man coverage. The Sam can now play his normal Hitman technique. However, if a #2 releases to Sam's side, Sam has the #2 with Man-to-Man coverage.

The Mike, seeing his key step to the weak side, begins flowing to the play side. Mike is free to the ball when his key goes to the weak side in Split. The setback, seeing the tackle block the E to the inside, steps around the tackle and up to the next level to meet the Mike. The setback ends up between the Mike and the ball. The Mike goes through the face of the setback and forces the blocker wider than the setback wants to be. The fullback, reading the block of the setback, takes the play to the outside, wider than he would like.

The Will (playside OLB) blitzes into the C gap. As the Will executes his blitz, he is reading the backfield action to alter his path as necessary.

DIAGRAM 4-6

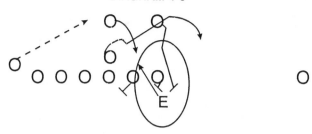

Because of the threat of Belly Option, the Will does not let himself get deeper than the quarterback, who is his responsibility on the Belly Option. Since the Will is responsible for the quarterback, he rarely steps inside to make the play. If the Will does tackle the fullback, the offensive coordinator could attempt the Belly Option on the next play to take advantage of the Will. If the Will does tackle the fullback, the Split Call should never be employed on the next play.

The playside C and the offside C are in Man-to-Man coverage and are not expected to get into the the play until very late. Since the wing went in motion, the offside C covers the tight end.

The SS (offside S) begins dropping into the deep middle zone and does not react to run until the threat of a passing play is gone. When the SS does react to the Belly, he becomes the Alley Player and slowly attacks the play from the inside-out.

DIAGRAM 4-7

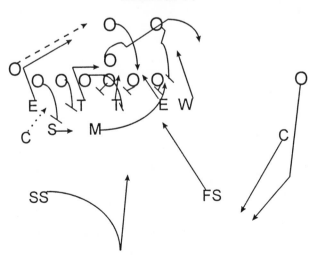

The FS (playside S), assuming his role as the pseudo-linebacker, begins to cheat up prior to the snap of the ball. Seeing two offensive backs attacking the B gap, the FS, like the Will in the Base 4–3, attacks the play from the outside-in. If only one offensive back attacks the B gap, the FS hangs outside and is prepared to cover the offensive back expecting the pitch in the Belly Option. (Diagram 4-7)

Key Blitz with He-Man Coverage

The strongside E (offside E) slants to the near eye of the offside tackle. The tackle steps toward the play side in an attempt to seal the offside B gap. The E steps into the tackle and pushes the tackle into the B gap. The E is in a good position if the fullback breaks back to the offside.

The strongside T (offside T) slants to the near eye of the center. With his momentum going toward the play side, the T meets the center as the center is trying to block him, and the E drives him into the playside A gap. A stalemate is unacceptable in this situation. The T is expected to move the center toward the play side and be in position for a cutback by the fullback.

The weakside T (playside T) does the exactly the same thing in Key Blitz that he does in Split.

The weakside E (offside E) slants to the near eye of the playside guard. As in Split, the playside tackle should attempt to block the slanting E to the inside. If the tackle can block the E (and he should be able to accomplish this block), the blocking scheme forces the setback to block outside the block of the tackle. When the E sees the playside guard block to the inside, he expects a down block by the tackle and should be ready to fight back, through the face of the tackle, toward the play.

The Sam (offside OLB) sees his key step away and sees no offensive player cross the Spot, opposite the direction of the key. The Sam assumes his Hitman technique and slowly flows toward the play, looking for a cutback by the fullback.

The Mike observes the key step toward the split-end side of the formation and the Mike immediately flows to the play side. Mike does not blitz in Key Blitz when the ball goes to the weak side. Seeing the tackle block down on the E into the B gap, the Mike continues to flow to the outside and does not allow a gap to develop between himself and the down block of the tackle. The closeness of the blitz to the tackle's block prevents the setback from turning the Mike to the outside and leaving a big hole to the inside for the fullback. (Diagram 4-8) The Mike, with momentum on his side, attacks the blocking setback and drives him into the backfield, either making the play on the fullback or, at least, forcing the fullback to break to the outside.

The Will (playside OLB) blitzes the C gap as he sees his key step playside. As in Split, the Will has responsibility for the quarterback on Belly Option or Belly Pass, and the Will does not get deeper than the quarterback.

DIAGRAM 4-8

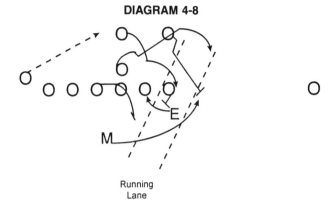

Running
Lane

The Will is not expected to make the play, but, if the fullback is driven wide by the attack of the Mike on the setback, the Will may, and often does, make the play.

The playside and offside C's do the same thing they do in Orange Spy coverage. They cover #1, to their side, Man-to-Man.

The SS (offside S) with only one receiver to his side after the wing goes in motion, becomes an FS and begins to drop into the deep middle area. However, if a #2 releases to the side of the SS, the SS takes the #2 with Man-to-Man coverage. As in Orange Spy, when he recognizes run, he cautiously attacks the play from the inside-out and becomes the Alley Player.

DIAGRAM 4-9

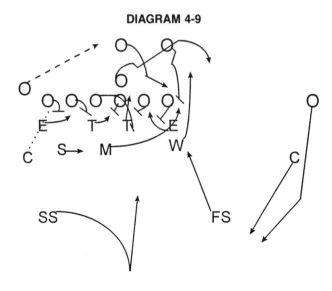

The FS (playside S) observes #2 move toward the LOS. The FS starts up to meet the setback (#2). The FS comes to the LOS and attacks the play from the inside-out. With no offensive player remaining to block the FS, the FS normally makes the play. (Diagram 4-9)

HB COUNTER

The HB Counter is a true misdirection running play in the Wing-T Offense. This is one play where correct reading of the Spot by the linebackers is the real key to successfully stopping the play.

Base 4–3 with Green Coverage

Again, in a definite running down situation, the secondary would declare strength to the wing/tight-end side. However, wing motion could make the secondary change the strength call to the direction of the motion. In this description, the secondary, again, changes the strength call with the wing motion.

The strongside E (playside E) attacks the tight end as the tight end attempts to cut off the E. The E, prior to getting into his trail mode, sees the setback coming back on the Counter and fights through the face of the tight end, forcing the tight end into the C gap. The E is in a good position when the setback spills to the outside.

Like the Trap, the strongside T (playside T) is the key to stopping the HB Counter. The T attacks the playside guard as the guard releases to the inside to block the Mike. The T gets a good piece of the guard to prevent the guard from having a clean shot at the Mike. As the guard releases to the inside, the T steps with his outside foot, making his shoulders nearly parallel to the LOS. The inside release of the guard indicates to the T the strong possibility of the trap-blocking scheme. The T attacks the trapping offside tackle. Unlike the Guard Trap, the T has a longer period of time to react to and attack the offside tackle. The T *attacks* the offside trapping tackle and wrong shoulders the blocker. The Wrong Shoulder forces the setback (halfback) to spill to the outside.

The weakside T (offside T) plays the Counter blocking scheme in the same manner that he plays the Trap. The T cannot allow the center to block him to the offside or off the ball. The T fights through the face of the center, forcing the center into the playside A gap and, along with the playside T using the Wrong Shoulder, restricts the playside A and B gaps.

The weakside E (offside E) attacks the offside tackle and reads the tackle's pull to the play side. Recognizing the blocking scheme, the E knows the fullback is coming to block him. The E cannot, however, fly down the line with the tackle pull. The quarterback may execute the Counter Bootleg,

DIAGRAM 4-10

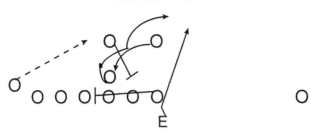

and the E is responsible for containing the quarterback on this play. The E rarely makes the play on the HB Counter but normally does make the play on the Counter Bootleg. (Diagram 4-10)

The setback (ballcarrier) rocks his weight to the weak side prior to stepping toward the quarterback to get the handoff. The three linebackers take their time to read the actual step of the setback and *not* his shoulder movement. Time must be taken in practice to teach the linebackers how to correctly read the various movements of the Wing-T setback. In this discussion, it is assumed the linebackers read the setback moving toward the tight-end side and, when reading the Spot, observe the offside offensive tackle crossing it in the same direction as the key (setback).

The Sam (playside OLB) is attacked by the playside tackle who tries to cut the Sam off from the play. The Sam fights through the face of the tackle and pushes the tackle into the B gap. The Sam often makes the play when the setback is forced to spill to the outside. For this reason, it is imperative for the Sam not to cross the face of the tackle and give the setback a lane in which to run.

The Mike steps up toward the A gap where he meets the playside guard attempting to block him to the inside. When the playside T does a good job of getting a piece of the guard, the Mike has a good amount of time to react to the attack of the guard. The Mike fights through the face of the guard as he pushes the guard into the B gap.

The Will, as the Hitman, begins his movement toward the play side. With the fullback picking up the offside E, who is slowly moving to the play side with the offside tackle pull, the offside guard sets his sights on the Will. The guard has an excellent angle on the Will and can easily come between the Will and the ballcarrier. Since the Will is looking for a cutback, he attempts to force the guard into the A gap but remains aware of his cutback responsibility. The Will makes a play on the ballcarrier only if the setback cuts to the offside or when the Will is in his proper pursuit angle.

The secondary, reacting to the wing motion, rotates in the same manner that it did versus the Belly. The SS (playside safety) has the last

DIAGRAM 4-11

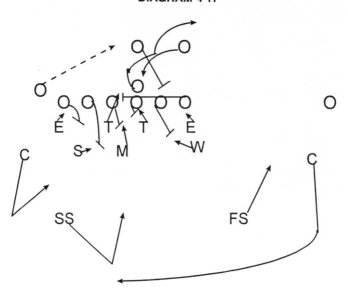

good shot at the ballcarrier if he breaks through the LOS on the play side. (Diagram 4-11)

At this point it is important to reemphasize two very significant elements in stopping the Trap and the HB Counter plays with the Base 4–3 Defense. The attack by the playside T on the playside offensive guard is critical to successfully halting both plays. The T *must* make good contact with the guard to prevent the guard from getting an unencumbered shot at the Mike. The playside guard has a good angle on the Mike and is able to make contact with him. The attack by the T hampers the guard's release and gives the Mike a much better chance to get in on the play. The attack by the playside T on the trapper and the Wrong Shoulder technique used by the T is, unquestionably, the most important part of stopping both plays. When the technique is done correctly, there is no hole for the ballcarrier and the Spill to the outside is his only alternative. The playside T is the central defender in stopping both Wing-T plays.

Split with Orange Spy Coverage

The strongside E (playside E) gap charges the strongside D gap. As in the Belly, the move of the E takes him away from the play. When the E realizes the Counter is being executed, he squeezes to the inside and gets into the proper pursuit angle to make the play downfield.

The strongside T (playside T) runs his gap charge through the playside B gap, opening up a natural hole for the setback. As in the Trap, the job of the T is to recognize the Counter and quickly squeeze to the inside to force the pulling offside tackle to attempt to block him. With the offside tackle pulling, instead of the offside guard in Trap, the playside T has a bit more time to recognize the play and react to the inside. As in the Base 4–3, the T is to wrong shoulder the trapper in an attempt to force the setback (ballcarrier) to spill to the outside. At times in the Split the T does not have enough time to react back to wrong shoulder the trapper. If the T forces the trapper to take him and not go up into the hole, the T has performed an adequate, but certainly not outstanding, job.

The weakside T (offside T) attacks the offside A gap. Since the offside guard is prepared to block the Will and the offside tackle is pulling, there is a good chance the T can collide with the pulling offside tackle. With the fullback concentrating on sealing the offside B gap and blocking the E, the T has a good chance of breaking through and stopping the play. (Diagram 4-12)

The weakside E (offside E) executes his gap charge through the offside B gap. The E is the key defender in stopping the play. The gap-charging E collides with the pulling tackle and totally disrupts the tackle's path. Even if the offside guard sees the E gap charge the B gap, it is too late for the guard to stop him. Remember, versus the 4–3 Defense, the guard expects to go to the next level and pick up the Will and expects the fullback to take the E. The collision of the E with the pulling tackle also causes problems for the fullback. He may either attack the E or see the blitzing Will and go to block him. Either way, the E either destroys the play or, at least, totally disrupts the blocks of the pulling tackle and the fullback. In Split, the E does not have to worry about the quarterback in Counter Bootleg (Will's responsibility) and he can aggressively fly to the inside. (Diagram 4-13)

DIAGRAM 4-12

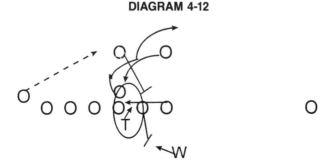

DIAGRAM 4-13

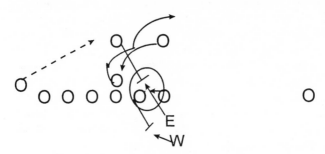

The Sam (playside OLB) sees the tackle attempt to cut him off. Since the Sam is responsible for the C gap and is no longer responsible for covering the tight end (wing motion), he fights through the face of the tackle and forces the tackle into the playside B gap. The Sam cannot go across the face of the tackle, as this would leave the playside C gap open and the setback could run there if the playside T forces the back to spill outside.

The Mike plays the HB Counter in the same way that he plays the Trap in the Split Defense. The Mike knows the playside guard is untouched, and the Mike attacks the guard and pushes him into the B gap.

The Will (offside OLB) blitzes the offside C gap. Because of the threat of Counter Bootleg, the Will does not get deeper than the quarterback. In

DIAGRAM 4-14

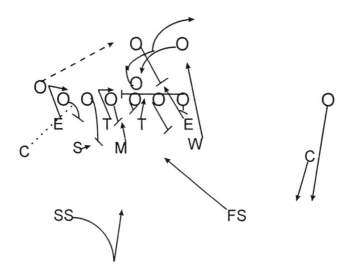

Split, the Will is responsible for the quarterback in Belly Option, Belly Pass, and Counter Bootleg. It is rare for the Will to make the play on the HB Counter.

The playside C and the offside C are in Man-to-Man coverage and are not expected to get into the play until very late. Since the wing went in motion, the offside C covers the tight end.

The SS (playside S) begins his drop into the deep middle zone. When he recognizes run, he slowly reacts to it as the Alley Player.

The FS (offside S), becoming the pseudo-linebacker, cheats up prior to the snap of the ball. While looking for #2 releasing, he hesitates momentarily to be sure the fullback is not releasing into the flat on Counter Bootleg. Once he recognizes the HB Counter, he moves to the play side to make the tackle. He may have to beat the block of the offside guard to be in on the play. However, if the FS effectively hides his approach to the LOS, the guard does not see him and the FS may end up unblocked. (Diagram 4-14)

Key Blitz with He-Man Coverage

The strongside E (playside E) slants to the near eye of the playside tackle. The tight end, attempting to cut off the E, may get a piece of him but the tight end cannot prevent the E from getting inside. The E reacts to the HB Counter in the same way that he reacts to the Trap. The E attacks the offside tackle as the tackle attempts to block the E. Since the presnap alignment of the offside tackle is wider than the alignment of the offside guard, the E has more time to react to the attempted block of the tackle than the E had versus the guard in the Trap. The Wrong Shoulder attack by the E forces the setback (ballcarrier) to spill to the outside.

The strongside T (playside T) slants to the near eye of the center. The scenario for the playside T and the playside guard is the same as the Trap. The guard may opt to block the T as the T crosses his face and leave the Mike unblocked, or the guard may leave the T unblocked and go to the next level to block the Mike. In either case, the unblocked Mike or the unblocked T can stop the play. The playside guard has a real dilemma. If he blocks the T, the Mike is left unblocked and can easily make the play. If the guard bypasses the T and blocks the Mike, the T is in a great position to force the trapper to attempt the trap block in the offside A gap, and this is not the place where the play is expected to develop. This can stop the HB Counter before it gets a real chance to start. (Diagram 4-15)

The weakside T (offside T) does exactly the same thing in Key Blitz that he does in Split.

The weakside E slants to the near eye of the offside guard. The slanting E should get a piece of the guard and keep him from quickly getting to the Will (Hitman). If the guard stays with, and attempts to block, the E, the fullback goes after the Will. With momentum and the offside

DIAGRAM 4-15

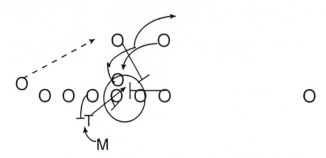

guard not expecting the E in his face, the E has an excellent chance to make the play.

The Sam (playside OLB), on the movement of his key, blitzes the D gap and is in a good position to make the play only when the setback spills to the outside.

The Mike, blitzing the playside B gap, may encounter the playside guard or the playside tackle. The playside guard is normally not quick enough to get to the Mike and may go to the offside or downfield. The playside tackle, who attempts to get the Sam but sees the Sam go away from the play, goes to the next level and views the Mike blitzing into the B gap. The tackle, if quick enough, can alter his path and attempt to get the Mike. (Diagram 4-16)

The Will (offside OLB) becomes the Hitman but must hold for the Counter Bootleg before he can flow toward the ball. On Counter Bootleg, the Will has the quarterback and cannot take the chance of allowing the quarterback to turn the corner. This delay gives the fullback the possibility of a good block on the Will. The Will expects the fullback's block and is

DIAGRAM 4-16

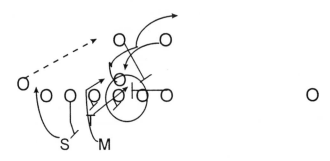

DIAGRAM 4-17

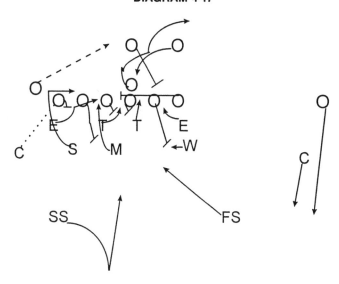

ready to attack it and push the fullback to the inside. Although the Will's delay can cause defensive problems on the HB Counter, it is necessary in order to stop the Counter Bootleg.

The playside and offside C's do the same thing that they do in Orange Spy coverage. They cover #1 to their side, Man-to-Man.

The SS (offside S), with only one receiver to his side after the wing goes in motion, becomes an FS and begins to drop into the deep middle area. If a #2 releases to his side, the SS covers him with Man-to-Man coverage. As in Orange Spy, when he recognizes run, he cautiously attacks the play from the inside-out and becomes the Alley Player.

The FS (playside S) sees the fullback attack the LOS and recognizes the possibility of the fullback becoming #2. When all threat of pass has gone, the FS attacks the play from the inside-out and often makes the play. (Diagram 4-17)

KEY POINTS TO STOPPING THE BELLY

Base

1. The playside T cannot allow himself to be collapsed to the inside, and the playside E cannot allow himself to be driven outside.

2. The Will must attack the B gap when he sees two backs go into it.

3. The Mike has to jam the lead blocker into the B gap.

Split

1. The Mike must force the lead blocker wider than the setback wants to be.
2. The FS must quickly recognize the running play and attack the play from the outside-in.

Key Blitz

1. The Mike must blitz as close to the down block of the playside tackle as possible.
2. The FS has to come up and take the play from the inside-out.

KEY POINTS TO STOPPING THE HB COUNTER

Base

1. The playside T must get a good piece of the playside guard to keep the guard from quickly releasing on the Mike.
2. The playside T must wrong shoulder the pulling offside tackle.
3. The Mike must push the playside guard into the B gap.

Split

1. The offside E must get into the B gap and disrupt the pulling tackle.
2. The Mike must recognize the blocking scheme and not allow the playside guard to pin him inside.
3. The playside T must react back and force the pulling tackle to block him.

Key Blitz

1. The playside E must force the pulling tackle to block him.
2. The FS must react up to the run and attack it from the outside-in.
3. The playside tackle must get a piece of the pulling tackle and knock the tackle off his path.

Chapter 5

Defending the Belly Option and Sprint Option

BELLY OPTION

The Wing-T executes the Belly Option from various formations. For the purpose of this discussion, the wing formation, with wing motion, is described. This allows the reader to more readily see the similarities in executing the Belly (Chapter 4), the HB Counter (Chapter 4), and the Belly Option and the similarities in defending against these plays.

Base 4–3 with Green Coverage

In the descriptions of the Belly and HB Counter (Chapter 4), the secondary changed the strength call with wing motion. That practice continues in this discussion of the Belly Option.

The strongside E (offside E) attacks the tight end and is sure to get a good piece of the tight end to prevent the tight end from getting downfield and cutting off one of the safeties. The E observes the play go to the opposite side and the E trails the play, looking for Counter or Reverse.

The strongside T (offside T) attacks the strongside guard and reads the guard's attempt to cut him off. The T fights through the face of the guard and pushes the guard into the offside A gap. When the T recognizes the Belly Option, he gets into the proper pursuit angle and flows toward the play.

The weakside T (playside T) attacks the center and is often blocked by the center and the playside guard. The playside guard executes a "Chip" block on the T and then goes to the next level to pick off the Mike. The guard attempts to push the T into the center's block to allow the center to cut off the T. When the T feels the guard, he fights in the direction of the guard and

DIAGRAM 5-1

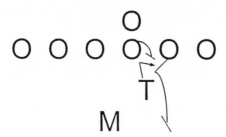

grabs the guard to disrupt his path to the next level. (Diagram 5-1) This "Grabbing" takes the T away from the center's block and allows the T to flow playside. Often, the T ends up running into the fullback.

The weakside E (playside E) attacks the playside tackle and feels the tackle's attempted reach block. The E fights the block and keeps outside leverage on the blocker. The reach block tells the E the play is going to the outside. However, the E cannot allow himself to get too wide, as a natural hole opens up inside and the quarterback could follow the fullback up and through the hole. (Diagram 5-2) Keeping outside leverage, the E takes the quarterback if he turns up with the ball. When the quarterback pitches to the back, the E breaks on the correct pursuit angle to intercept the ballcarrier after the ballcarrier crosses the LOS.

The Sam (offside OLB) sees his key step to the weak side, and observes no offensive player cross the Spot to the strong side. The Sam becomes the Hitman and slowly flows toward the play, avoiding the cutoff attempt by the offside tackle.

The Mike reads the setback step to the weak side and sees no offensive player cross the Spot toward the strong side. The Mike flows to the

DIAGRAM 5-2

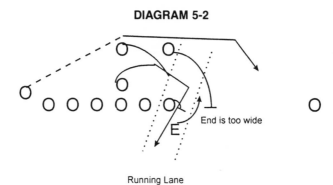

End is too wide

Running Lane

playside B gap. He meets the offside guard after the guard chips off the playside T. The Mike attacks the guard and drives the guard into the playside B gap. There are times when the Mike's quickness, along with the playside T grabbing the playside guard, enables the Mike to beat the guard's block. When this occurs, the fullback comes outside the offside tackle's block and attempts to seal the Mike to the inside. The Mike fights through the face of the fullback and drives toward the ball. (Diagram 5-3)

The Will (playside OLB) sees only one back (fullback) go toward the playside B gap. The Will steps to the outside and is responsible for the D gap and the back receiving the pitch. The setback attacks the Will and intends to block the Will to the inside. In collegiate football, the setback is allowed to cut the Will, and this is the most difficult block for the Will to defeat. The Will cannot allow the setback to get to his legs, and the Will keeps his hands in front and low to meet the blocker and stay outside the blocker. In scholastic football, the setback is not allowed to cut block and must block above the knees of the Will. This is a simpler block for the Will to defend. The Will attacks the outside shoulder of the blocker and rips through the block. When the motion back receives the pitch, the Will slides along the LOS and attempts to stay on the outside shoulder of the pitchman. This outside leverage, on the LOS position, gives the Will the opportunity to tackle the ballcarrier if the ballcarrier continues to the outside or cuts back to the inside. The Will is *never* expected to make the tackle on the offensive side of the LOS.

The SS (offside S), with the change of strength, becomes the FS and begins to rotate to the deep middle one-third zone. On recognition of Belly Option, the SS becomes the Alley Player and is expected to tackle the quarterback if the quarterback keeps the ball and turns up inside.

The FS (playside S), with the change of strength, becomes the SS and rotates up through the curl area to the flat. With the strong rotation, the SS becomes an extra defender to the ball. Versus most Wing-T Belly Options, the FS comes up and is an additional defender on the pitchman. However,

DIAGRAM 5-3

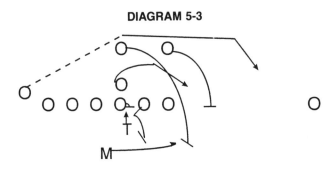

DIAGRAM 5-4

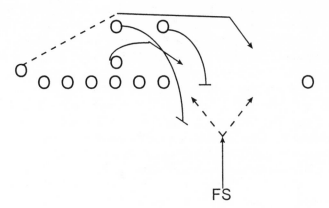

when the offense employs a quarterback who is a greater running threat than the halfback, the FS can be assigned to cautiously flow to a position several yards outside the quarterback and 4 to 5 yards off the LOS. From this vantage point, the FS can jump the quarterback if the quarterback gets outside the E and keeps the ball, or he can attack the pitchman if the pitchman receives the ball. (Diagram 5-4)

DIAGRAM 5-5

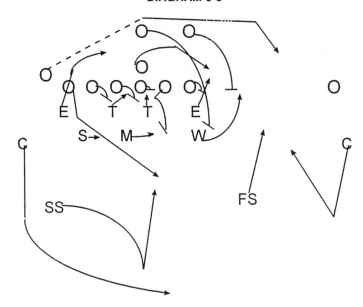

The C (offside C) drops to the deep outside one-third zone. When he recognizes weakside run, the C carefully rotates through the deep middle zone, looking for cutback.

The C (playside) begins to drop to the deep outside one-third zone. When he recognizes a run and is sure all threat of a pass is gone, the C attacks the play from the outside-in. (Diagram 5-5)

Split with Orange Spy Coverage

The strongside E (offside E) charges through the strongside D gap. The gap charge takes the E away from the play. When the E recognizes that the play is being executed away from him, he checks for Waggle and then trails the play, looking for Counter or Reverse.

The strongside T (offside T) gap charges through the offside B gap. The offside tackle, who is stepping through the B gap to flow to the Sam, makes contact with the T and tries to get between the T and the play. The T attacks the tackle and fights to prevent the tackle from cutting him off. The T gets in the proper pursuit angle and breaks toward the play side.

The weakside T (playside T) gap charges the playside A gap. As in the Base 4–3, both the center and the playside guard initially attack the T. Again, the playside guard chips the T and then goes to the next level to block the Mike. When the T is quick enough and the playside guard does not step at the correct angle to attack a gap-charging defender, the T does get through the LOS and either tackles the quarterback or, at least, collides with the fullback. This excellent play by the T does rarely occur but cannot be counted upon to stop the play. (Diagram 5-6)

The weakside E (playside E) attacks the playside B gap. The playside tackle, stepping to the play side, must quickly react back to block the E. Just as the playside T does rarely make a great play, beating the playside guard, the playside E, on occasion, makes a great play and stops the quarterback in the backfield for a loss. Most often, the E fights through the block of the tackle and gets into the proper pursuit angle to get in on the play.

DIAGRAM 5-6

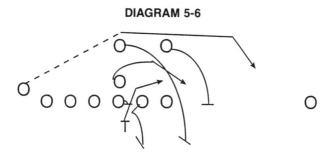

From this point on in this chapter, it is understood that the three linebackers read their setback key and see him flow to the weak side versus the Belly Option and to the strong side versus the Sprint Option. Furthermore, it is understood no offensive player crosses the Spot in a direction opposite the key.

The Sam (offside OLB), with wing motion, no longer has the tight end with Man-to-Man coverage. The Sam becomes the Hitman and flows toward the play side. The Sam remains aware of the possibility of a #2 releasing to his side. Since the offside tackle picked up the gap-charging playside T, the offside guard steps up to block the Sam and keep him away from the play. The Sam fights through the guard and gets into the proper pursuit angle to stop the play.

The Mike flows toward the play side. He meets the offside guard after the guard chips off the playside T. The Mike attacks the guard and drives the guard into the playside B gap. The Mike fights through the face of the fullback and drives, at the correct pursuit angle, toward the ball.

The Will (playside OLB) blitzes the C. After avoiding the fullback, the Will immediately attacks the quarterback. This quick attack results either in the Will tackling the quarterback for a loss or in an extremely quick pitch by the quarterback. This is one situation where the Will is coached to really "Smash" the quarterback. The blitzing Will, blitzing at top speed, has little chance of stopping the blitz and getting in the correct pursuit angle to have a play on the pitchman. For this reason, the Will is expected to make the quarterback pay a high price for the premature pitch. A few good shots like this and the quarterback will want to quickly pitch on every Belly Option to avoid the crushing hit by the Will. (Diagram 5-7)

Orange Spy Coverage is not the best coverage to successfully stop an Option Play. However, with the quick attack by the Will on the quarterback, a quick pitch is the result, and this gives the FS a good amount of time to get to the lead blocker and either tackle the pitchman or force the ballcarrier to the inside and into the jaws of the pursuit.

DIAGRAM 5-7

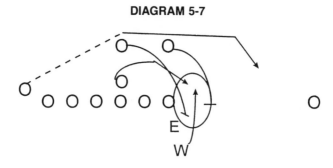

DIAGRAM 5-8

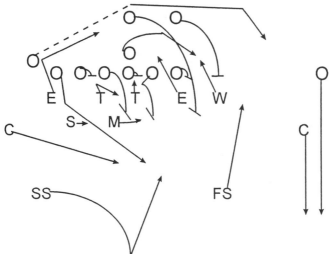

The SS (offside S) rotates into the deep middle zone. When he recognizes the Belly Option and is sure all possibilities of a passing play are gone, he becomes the Alley Player and looks for the quarterback keeping the ball.

The FS (playside S) moves toward the LOS and recognizes the Belly Option. Since the Will quickly attacked the quarterback, a very quick pitch is the result. The FS attacks the setback (attempting a cut block) and keeps outside leverage on him. The FS cannot allow the pitchman to get outside as there is no defender out there to help. When the FS forces the ballcarrier inside, the SS, along with other pursuing defenders, is in good position to tackle the pitchman.

The playside and offside corners are in Man-to-Man coverage and are not expected to get into the play until the pitchman crosses the LOS. (Diagram 5-8)

Key Blitz with He-Man Coverage

The strongside E (offside E) executes his slant to the near eye of the offside tackle. The offside tackle is stepping through the offside B gap on his way to cut the Sam off from the play. When the tackle sees the slanting E, the tackle stays on the LOS and attempts to cut off the E. The E fights through the face of the tackle and gets into the proper pursuit angle.

The strongside T (offside E) slants to the near eye of the center. The offside guard, stepping into the offside A gap, attempts to cut the T off from

DIAGRAM 5-9

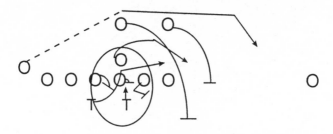

the play. The offside guard gets a piece of the T but, normally, cannot prevent the T from getting to the play side. If a hole opens, prior to the T hitting the center who is blocking the playside T, the offside T shoots the hole and could cause some problems in the offensive backfield. (Diagram 5-9)

The weakside T (playside T) does the same thing on Key Blitz that he does in Split, and the center and offside guard react in the same manner.

The weakside E (playside E) slants to the near eye of the offside guard. This move by the E forces the playside guard to quickly come off the Chip block on the playside T and attempt to block the playside E. There are times when the playside guard is not quick enough to pick up the playside E and the E gets into the backfield and causes a problem for the backs. This is normally not enough to stop the play. The offside tackle, who normally blocks the E, goes to the next level and looks for the Mike.

The Sam (offside OLB) assumes his Hitman technique and slowly flows toward the play. The Sam gets into the proper pursuit angle and often makes the play when the FS forces the pitchman to cut back to the inside.

The Mike flows to the play side and meets the playside tackle who bypassed the slanting E to block on the next level. The Mike fights through the face of the tackle and does not allow himself to be pinned inside. When the Mike gets through the tackle, he meets the blocking fullback and also fights through his block.

The Will blitzes the C gap and reacts in the same way that he reacted in the Split. The Will either tackles the quarterback or forces a very quick pitch to the trailing halfback.

The SS (offside S) starts to rotate into the deep middle zone and makes sure no #2 releases to his side. When he recognizes the Belly Option, and is sure all possibilities of a passing play are gone, he becomes the Alley Player and looks for the quarterback keeping the ball.

The FS (playside S) moves toward the LOS and sees #2 (setback) arc release and the FS recognizes the Belly Option. Since the Will quickly

DIAGRAM 5-10

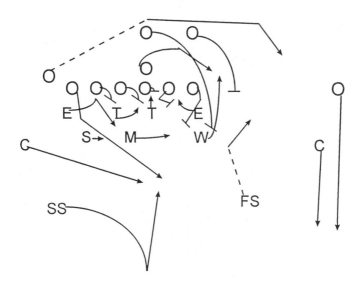

attacked the quarterback, a very quick pitch is the result. As in Split, the FS attacks the setback (who is attempting a cut block) and keeps outside leverage on him. The FS cannot allow the pitchman to get outside as there is no defender out there to help. When the FS forces the ballcarrier inside, the SS, along with other pursuing defenders, is in good position to tackle the pitchman.

The playside and offside corners are in Man-to-Man coverage and are not expected to get into the play until the pitchman crosses the LOS. (Diagram 5-10)

SPRINT OPTION

The Sprint Option is often run when the offensive coordinator recognizes the tendency of the defense to rotate the secondary to the slot side of the formation. The 4–3 Defense, even with the secondary rotating away from the play side, is still capable of effectively stopping the Sprint Option. The Split and Key Blitz are the more effective defensive schemes versus the Sprint Option, but the Base also works well.

Base 4–3 with Green Coverage

The strongside E (playside E) attacks the tight end and opens with his outside foot until he is sure the release of the tight end is an arc release and not an attempt to execute a reach block on the E. The E sees the setback release and the E, remaining on the LOS, fights to keep outside leverage on the blocker. The E is responsible for the pitchman and cannot allow himself to be cut or blocked inside by the setback. The E attacks the outside shoulder of the setback and never allows the setback outside leverage.

The strongside T (playside T) attacks the playside guard and feels the guard's attempt to cut off the T. The T fights through the face of the guard, forcing the guard into the playside B gap. When the T realizes the play is the Sprint Option, he gets into the correct pursuit angle and sprints to the outside. Pursuit is extremely important versus all plays but critical versus the Sprint Option.

The weakside T attacks the center and, like the playside T, feels the attempted cutoff block by the offside guard. Normally, the center "Punches" the T and attempts to set the T up for a cutoff block by the offside guard. The center then goes through the playside A gap, attempting to pick any penetration in that area. The T fights through the face of the guard and gets into his pursuit angle as quickly as possible.

The weakside E (offside E) employs his normal alignment versus a slot. The E attacks the tackle and fights through the tackle's attempted cutoff block. When the E recognizes Sprint Option away from the weak side, he gets into the proper pursuit angle.

The Sam (playside OLB) reads his key (setback) and the quarterback sprint to the outside. The Sam also observes the arc release of the tight end. As the C-gap player, the E is responsible for the quarterback on the Sprint Option. The E easily steps outside the attempted cutoff by the playside tackle and employs the "Cat" technique on the quarterback. The Cat technique involves the Sam remaining at least 3 yards off the LOS and on the outside shoulder of the quarterback. Having the Sam execute this technique does not give the quarterback a good "Keep or Pitch" read. The Cat technique produces several beneficial results for the defense. The quarterback, having trouble making a decision, gives the pursuing defensive personnel a chance to get to the play. If the quarterback turns upfield to run the ball, the Sam can fall inside and attack the quarterback for a small gain. If the quarterback pitches the ball, the depth of the Sam allows the Sam to attack the pitchman and the Sam becomes an extra man to the ball. The Cat technique works extremely well but it takes a disciplined Sam and a great deal of practice time.

The Mike, seeing the Sprint Option, can be much less concerned about the playside B gap. Seeing full flow going to the outside nearly eliminates the possibility of an offensive attack at the playside B gap. The Mike fights through the face of the playside tackle and gets into the proper pursuit angle.

The Will (offside OLB), versus a slot, employs his normal weakside

DIAGRAM 5-11

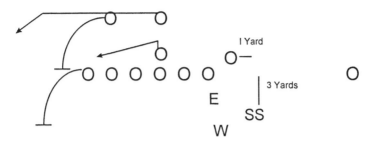

alignment and assumes his role of Hitman. However, with full flow going away and no wide receiver to run a Reverse, the Will sprints to the play side and looks for either the quarterback or the pitchman cutting back. The offside T attempts to cut off the Will but cannot get to him.

Versus the slot formation, using Green coverage, an adjustment is made in the secondary alignment. The corners maintain their normal alignment but the safeties alter their alignments. Since the Will is outflanked by the slot, the SS is moved up or pre-rotates prior to the snap. The SS's basic position is 1 yard outside the slot and 3 yards deep. If the slot splits wider than a normal tight end, the SS moves out with the slot and the SS adjusts his alignment to the inside to prevent a quick inside pass pattern by the slot. The alignment of the SS gives the appearance of an eight-man front. The FS moves to a position over the weakside guard and aligns as deep as the split end is aligned from the weakside tackle. If the split end is split 10 yards from the offensive tackle, the FS aligns 10 yards deep. (Diagram 5-11)

The FS (playside S) reads the play from his deep middle one-third zone and becomes the Alley Player when all threats of a pass disappear.

The SS (offside S) starts to drop to the curl area. When he is sure there is no possible offensive player who can threaten his area, he gets into the proper pursuit angle to attack the play.

The C (playside) covers the deep outside one-third zone and cannot come up until the ballcarrier crosses the LOS. The C is very aware of the possibility of an HB Option pass.

The C (offside) drops to the outside one-third zone. When he recognizes weakside run, the C rotates through the deep middle zone, looking for a cutback. (Diagram 5-12)

Split with Orange Spy Coverage

The strongside E (playside E) gap charges the playside D gap and is responsible for the quarterback. As soon as the E recognizes Sprint Option,

DIAGRAM 5-12

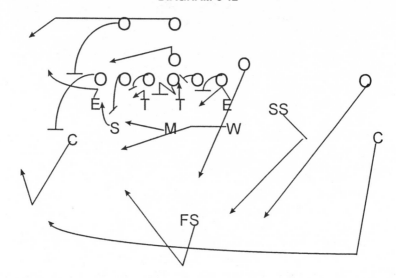

the E turns and attacks the quarterback. Remember, except for the weakside T, the gap charge is made under control and the E has no problem working inside to take the QB.

The strongside T (playside T) executes his gap charge through the playside B gap. Although the playside guard may get a piece of the T, he rarely cuts off the T. At times, the T does get through and makes a great play on the quarterback. This great play cannot be expected but, when it occurs, it really knocks the offense, and the quarterback, for a loop. (Diagram 5-13)

The weakside T (offside T) gap charges the offside A gap. Like the Base 4–3, the center punches the T and attempts to set the T up for a cutoff

DIAGRAM 5-13

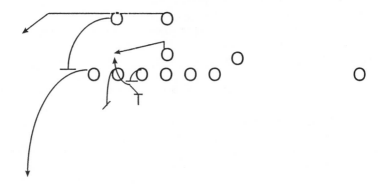

block by the offside guard. The center then goes through the playside A gap, attempting to pick any penetration in that area. The T fights through the face of the guard and gets into his pursuit angle as quickly as possible.

The weakside E (offside E) attacks the offside B gap. Like the playside T, there are times when the E beats the block of the tackle and gets into the backfield. However, when the E does get into the backfield, he is too far from the play to disrupt it and must get into his proper pursuit angle to have any hand in stopping the play.

The Sam (playside OLB) is responsible for #2 to his side and is ready to apply the Inside-Outside rule with the playside C. On action, the C makes a "Me-You" call to tell the Sam who is covering the tight end with Man-to-Man coverage. When the C makes a You call, the Sam runs with the tight end and the C comes up to attack the setback (#2) and take the pitchman. When the C makes a Me call, the C runs with the tight end and the Sam attacks the setback (#2) and takes the pitchman. Versus the Sprint Option, the Me call is the preferred call. This allows the better run defender to attack the lead blocker.

The Mike, seeing the Sprint Option and full flow going to the outside, nearly disregards the playside A gap as he flows to the outside. The Mike fights through the face of the playside tackle and gets into the proper pursuit angle.

The Will (offside OLB) blitzes the offside C gap. Upon recognition of the Sprint Option to the opposite side, the Will gets into the proper pursuit angle.

As in Green coverage, the secondary defenders alter their alignment to compensate for the slot formation. From the standpoint of the quarterback, the alignment of the secondary indicates Green but is actually in Orange Spy.

The SS (offside S) covers the slot (#2) with Man-to-Man coverage. Like the C's, the SS is not expected to get into the play until late.

The FS (onside S), from his deep middle one-third alignment, reacts to run only when the threat of a pass has disappeared. The FS becomes the Alley Player and looks for the quarterback running the ball.

Both C's are in Man-to-Man coverage with #1 to their side of the formation. (Diagram 5-14)

Key Blitz with He-Man Coverage

The strongside E (playside E) executes his slant to the near eye of the playside tackle. As the E slants, he recognizes the tackle attempting to seal the playside C gap. The E attacks the tackle but maintains outside leverage on the tackle. As soon as the E reads the Sprint Option he comes across the LOS and goes after the quarterback. The attack by the E normally forces a fast pitch. (Diagram 5-15)

DIAGRAM 5-14

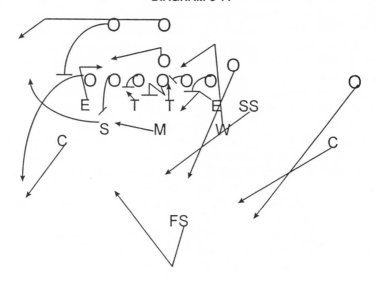

The strongside T (playside T) slants to the near eye of the center. Like the playside tackle, the center is stepping to the play side to protect the playside A gap. Like the playside E, the T attacks the center and maintains playside leverage on the center. Although the T may be able to beat the block of the center and get into the backfield, he is too late to get to the quarterback and gets into the proper pursuit angle and flows toward the ball.

The weakside T (offside T) does exactly the same thing in Key Blitz that he does in Split.

DIAGRAM 5-15

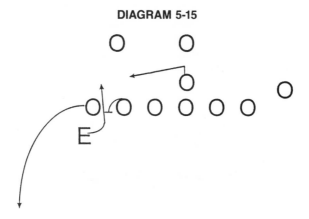

The weakside E (offside E) slants to the near eye of the offside guard. The E can often beat the cutoff block by the offside tackle but, like the playside T, the E is too late to get into the backfield to get the quarterback, and the E gets into the proper pursuit and moves toward the ball.

The Sam (playside OLB), responding to his key (setback), blitzes the playside D gap where he meets the setback. The setback attempts to pin the E to the inside but the E maintains outside leverage on the back and is ready to take the pitchman if the fullback gets the pitch.

The Mike blitzes the playside B gap and encounters the playside guard who is protecting the playside B gap. The Mike fights through the face of the guard but the Mike cannot get into the backfield soon enough to stop the play. However, with momentum on his side, the Mike gets into the proper pursuit angle and is normally in on the tackle.

The Will (offside OLB) assumes his Hitman technique. The Will looks for cutback and gets into his proper pursuit angle.

Both C's do exactly the same thing in He-Man coverage that they did in Orange Spy. The playside C covers the tight end with Man-to-Man coverage, and the offside C covers the split end with Man-to-Man coverage.

The SS (offside safety) covers the slot with Man-to-Man coverage and does not get involved with the running play until very late.

The FS (playside safety) sees # 2 release to the play side. The FS flows to the outside to be in position to take the setback (#2) if he releases for a pass. When the FS sees the setback attempt to block the Sam, the FS is in position to play the quarterback, if the E did not get him, or the pitchman. The FS becomes the extra man to the ball. (Diagram 5-16)

DIAGRAM 5-16

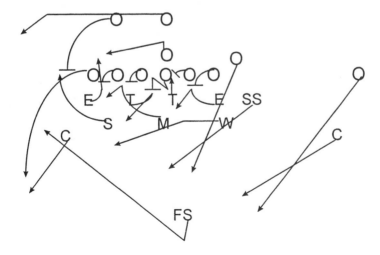

The quarterback, executing the Sprint Option against the Base 4–3, the Split, and the Key Blitz, sees three different Keep or Pitch keys. Versus the Base 4–3, the quarterback sees the Sam employing a Cat technique. Versus the Split, the quarterback sees the E, after the E gap charges the D gap, attack him. In Key Blitz, the quarterback is quickly attacked by the E, employing an inside slant move. These three defenses give the quarterback three different option reads and make it very difficult for the quarterback to get any real sense of how the defense plays the Sprint Option.

KEY POINTS TO STOPPING THE BELLY OPTION

The defender responsible for the pitch *cannot* get cut by the lead blocker!

Base

1. The end stays on the LOS and attacks the quarterback. The end cannot think about going inside for the Fullback fake.
2. The Will must keep outside leverage on the arc-blocking setback.
3. The FS has to be cautious and attack the player with the ball.

Split

1. The Will must put a punishing hit on the quarterback, either tackling the quarterback for a loss or forcing a fast pitch.
2. The FS must keep outside leverage on the lead blocker.
3. Defensive pursuit is critical on this play.

Key Blitz

1. Same as Split.

KEY POINTS TO STOPPING THE SPRINT OPTION

The defender responsible for the pitch *cannot* get cut by the lead blocker!

Base

1. The playside E must get outside to take the pitchman.
2. The Sam must use the Cat technique and not force a fast pitch.
3. The Mike has to be aggressive and not worry about the B gap.

Split

1. The E, after gap charging, has to get to the quarterback.

2. The C must make a Me-You call.

3. Whoever has the pitch responsibility must keep outside leverage on the lead blocker.

Key Blitz

1. The playside E must avoid the block of the playside tackle and attack the quarterback.

2. The FS has to be aggressive in coming up to the LOS.

3. The Sam must keep outside leverage on the lead blocker.

Chapter 6

Defending
the Waggle

The Wing-T Offense employs several excellent play-action passes. This chapter and the next cover the three most common play-action passes. These three plays are the Waggle, part of the Sweep series; the Belly Pass; and the Counter-Bootleg Pass, part of the Belly series. All three plays present different problems for the defense, and the 4–3 Defense is up to the task of effectively stopping both plays.

In this chapter, the defense expects the possibility of a pass and declares strength to the split-end side of the wing formation in Green coverage. Even when strength is declared to the wing side of the formation, the Base 4–3 with Green coverage is an effective defense versus the Waggle.

The Waggle is certainly the signature play-action passing play of the Wing-T Offense. The play forces the defense to cover all three deep zones and the flat areas to both sides of the offensive formation when playing zone coverage and five possible receivers when employing Man-to-Man coverages. In this chapter, the Waggle play is described from the wing formation, with the play being executed to the split-end side of the formation, and from the slot formation, with the play executed to the tight-end side of the formation. Although the Wing-T employs various pass patterns when using the Waggle, the following basic Waggle patterns are described and defended in this text:

To the split-end side of the Wing formation

- Wing — Step Inside, Deep Outside Route
- Tight End — Step Inside, Deep Crossing Route (reading the FS)
- Fullback — Block, if needed, or Flat Route
- Setback — Block or Flare Route
- Split End — Post Corner Route (Diagram 6-1)

DIAGRAM 6-1

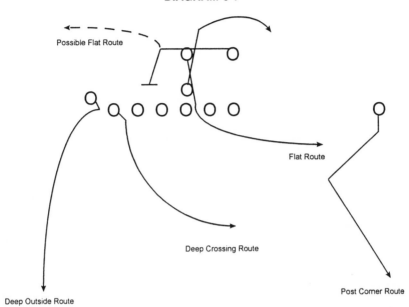

Possible Flat Route

Flat Route

Deep Crossing Route

Deep Outside Route

Post Corner Route

DIAGRAM 6-2

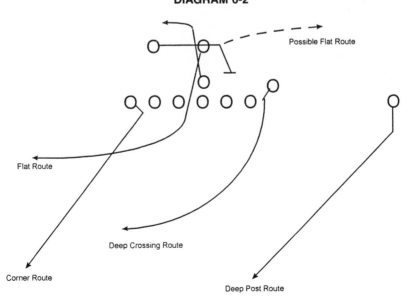

Possible Flat Route

Flat Route

Deep Crossing Route

Corner Route

Deep Post Route

To the tight-end side of the Slot formation

- Split End — Deep Post Route
- Slot — Step Inside, Deep Crossing Route
- Fullback — Block, if needed, or Flat Route
- Setback — Block or Flare Route
- Tight End — Step Inside, Corner Route (Diagram 6-2)

THE WAGGLE TO THE SPLIT-END SIDE

Base 4–3 with Green Coverage

The strongside E (offside E) attacks the tight end and reads the inside move of the tight end as an attempt to block inside. Like the Sweep, the E makes sure he gets a good piece of the tight end to prevent a block on the Sam or an easy release on a pass pattern. The E feels for the down block by the wing and the wing, depending on how he is coached, may step down to touch the E to influence the E to react to the outside. The wing may also take one step to the inside to simply influence the secondary into believing the Sweep is being executed. No matter what technique the wing employs, the E does not get a down block by the wing and sees no guards cross his face. The E quickly realizes it is not Sweep and looks for a possible Screen to the setback (faking Sweep) before getting into the proper pursuit angle. (Diagram 6-3)

DIAGRAM 6-3

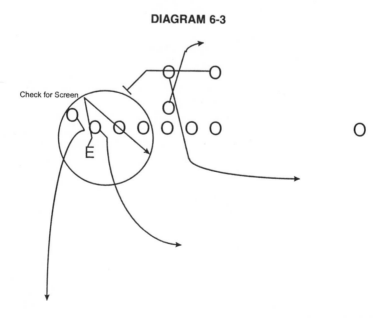

Check for Screen

The strongside T (offside T) attacks the guard and immediately reads the guard's weakside pull. The T steps with the pull and meets the center, who is cup blocking to the offside after using a Punch technique on the playside T. The T fights through the face of the center and gets into the proper pursuit angle.

The weakside T (playside T) attacks the center and feels the punch by the center and the down block by the playside tackle. The T fights through the face of the tackle and pushes the tackle into the playside C gap.

The weakside E (playside E) recognizes the inside move by the tackle. The E steps with his outside foot, and his shoulders become nearly perpendicular to the LOS. The E is looking for a Trap by the guard. The E sees the playside guard attempting to "Hook" him, and the E fights to keep outside leverage on the blocker. When the E does a good job, he remains outside the playside guard and forces the offside guard to block him. When this scenario occurs, the playside E has done an excellent job.

The Sam sees his key (setback) come to the strong side but sees the offside guard cross the Spot. The Sam knows it is not the Sweep and quickly recognizes Waggle. The E looks to the tight end and attempts to collide with him to prevent an unencumbered release into the secondary. There is no curl zone to the tight-end side and the E looks to his setback key for a possible flare or screen route. Even when the setback sets up to block, the E cannot drop deeper into the secondary until he is completely sure the setback is not going to slip out to the offside for a pass reception. When the E is sure the offside flat is not going to be attacked, he drops toward the deep middle and locates the ball.

The Mike views his key step to the strong side but then sees the offside guard cross the Spot. This action indicates Waggle to the Mike. The Mike turns and looks for the tight end running a crossing pattern. The Mike gets under the crossing pattern to prevent a completion to the tight end. The Mike continues to drop to keep a void area from developing between himself and the FS and giving the tight end a location for catching the ball. (Diagram 6-4)

The Will sees his key step to the strong side and sees the offside guard cross the Spot. The Will immediately thinks Waggle and realizes he has to blitz the C gap to stop the quarterback. The Will's reading of the Spot is the key to defending this play. Reading the Spot quickly alerts the Will to the Waggle and, hopefully, gives the Will enough time to beat the block of the offside guard and get to the quarterback. When the Will is not quick enough to beat the guard's block and get to the quarterback, he cannot allow himself to be pushed outside and, at least, must force the quarterback to "Pull Up" and not attack the corner. This Pullup can, at times, give the defensive linemen enough time to get to the quarterback.

If the offense changes the basic patterns and has the split end execute a curl instead of a post-corner route, the split end is open and, on the next

DIAGRAM 6-4

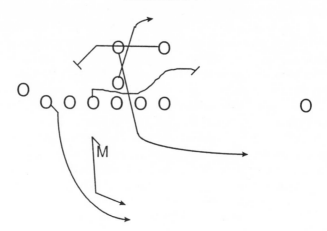

play, a different coverage has to be used or the Will has to be employed in the curl area (his basic Green coverage area of responsibility) and the blitz eliminated. (Diagram 6-5)

The SS (playside S) rotates through the curl area and picks up the fullback as the fullback runs the flat route. From his original alignment, the SS easily sees the fullback as the SS moves through the curl area. The SS does not go up to cover the fullback but hangs back to encourage the

DIAGRAM 6-5

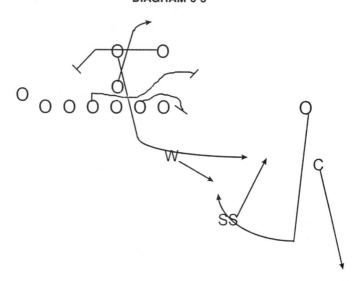

DIAGRAM 6-6

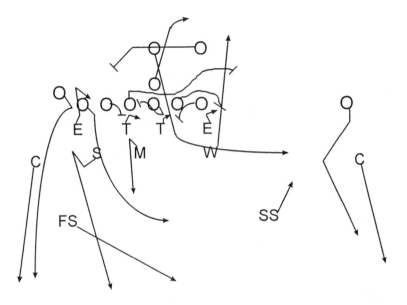

quarterback to throw the ball to the fullback. When this throw does occur, the SS is able to step in for the interception or breakup. If an interception or breakup is not possible, the SS is in a great position to smash the fullback and separate him from the ball.

The FS (offside S) rotates to the deep middle one-third zone. The FS keeps the tight end in front of him and the FS stays in good position to step up and intercept a ball thrown to the tight end. The FS cannot allow a large void to form between himself and the Mike. The tight end is looking for a void area to catch the ball.

The C (offside C) drops to the deep outside one-third zone and covers the wing running the deep outside route. When the quarterback decides to throw back to the wing, it is a very long pass and the C is in position to intercept it.

The C (playside C) drops to the deep outside one-third zone and covers the split end. (Diagram 6-6)

From this point on in this chapter, it is understood that the three linebackers read their normal key (setback) and then look to the Spot.

Split with Orange Spy Coverage

The strongside E (offside E) gap charges the D gap. This charge takes the E away from the play. However, when the E recognizes Waggle, he is in a good position to cover the setback on either a flare or screen route. When the ball is not thrown to the setback, the E gets into the proper pursuit angle.

The strongside T (offside T) gap charges the offside B gap. Seeing the offside guard pull, the T breaks in the direction of the pull and gets into the backfield. The offside tackle cannot prevent the T from moving toward the play side. The center, employing a cup-blocking technique, attempts to pick up the T. The T fights through the face of the center and gets into the proper pursuit angle.

The weakside T (playside T) fires through the playside A gap. The center tries to punch the T to set the T up for a block by the playside tackle. The T normally beats the block of the tackle with his gap charge and runs directly into the fullback who is sealing the playside A gap. The block by the fullback eliminates the fullback as a pass receiver. When the T gets to the fullback and forces a block, the T has done an excellent job. The T fights to the play side of the fullback and, at times, makes a great play on the quarterback when the Will forces the quarterback to pull up. (Diagram 6-7)

The weakside E (playside E) gap charges the playside B gap. The playside tackle, stepping down to the inside, makes contact with the E but rarely is quick enough to totally eliminate the penetration. If the E can get enough depth to collide with the offside pulling guard, the E is doing a great job.

The Sam (offside OLB) covers the tight end with Man-to-Man coverage. When the Sam sees the inside release by the tight end, the Sam collides with the tight end and intends to knock the tight end off his route. The Sam knows the FS is in the deep middle and the Sam depends upon the FS for deep help with the tight end. The deep help allows the Sam to play a very aggressive brand of Man-to-Man coverage.

The Mike, after reading his key and the Spot, recognizes the Waggle play. Since the SS, playing the pseudo-linebacker, covers #2 (fullback) to the play side and both #1 and #2 are covered to the play side and the offside, the Mike is available to cover #3 to either side. However, to the offside, the gap-charging (D gap) E is given the responsibility for #3 (setback) to that side on a flare or screen route. The Mike is left to

DIAGRAM 6-7

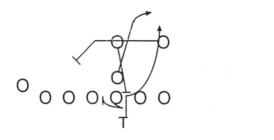

concentrate on the play side. There is no possibility of a playside #3 releasing for a pass, and this circumstance allows the Mike to blitz the quarterback and become an additional pass-rusher. The Mike can blitz through the first opening on the play side. Normally, the Mike executes his blitz in the C gap, following the blitz of the Will. The Mike could be attacked by the playside tackle. Since the playside T executes a gap charge and is picked up by the fullback, the tackle has no defender to block. Normally, by the time the playside tackle realizes he cannot block the T, the Mike is too far to the play side to be picked up by the tackle.

The Will (playside OLB) blitzes the C gap. Since the Will does not have to make a read to determine whether to blitz or not (as in the Base 4–3), the blitz is very fast, and this puts the Will in an excellent position to beat the block of the offside guard and get to the quarterback.

For the sake of consistency in this chapter, versus the wing set, in both Orange Spy and He-Man coverages, the SS aligns to the split-end side and the FS aligns to the tight-end/wing side of the formation. Of course, it is possible to reverse the alignment of the safeties, depending on the strengths and weaknesses of the Wing-T opponent.

The SS (playside S) moves toward the LOS and picks up #2 (the fullback) and covers him with Man-to-Man coverage.

The FS (offside S) rotates to the deep middle one-third zone. The FS reacts in the same manner that he reacted in the Green coverage. The FS keeps the tight end in front of him and the FS stays in good position to step up and intercept a ball to the tight end.

Both the playside C and the offside C cover #1, to their side, with Man-to-Man coverage. (Diagram 6-8)

DIAGRAM 6-8

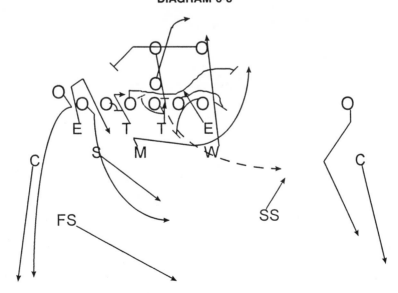

Key Blitz with He-Man Coverage

The strongside E (offside E) slants to the near eye of the offside tackle. The offside tackle is stepping to the inside to cut off the offside T, and the tackle's original position on the LOS is vacated. The E fills the area vacated by the tackle and the setback (faking Sweep) attacks him. However, when the E is quick enough to recognize the pulling offside guard and realize it is the Waggle, he can beat the setback and make a great play on the quarterback, especially when the quarterback is forced to pull up.

The strongside T (offside T) slants to the near eye of the center. Although the T is far enough from the cutoff attempt of the offside tackle, he runs directly into the cup-blocking center. The T fights through the face of the center and then gets into the proper pursuit angle.

The weakside T (playside T) does the same thing in the Key Blitz front that he does in Split front.

The weakside E (playside E) slants to the near eye of the playside guard. The playside tackle, stepping down to the inside, blocks the E to the inside. The E fights through the face of the tackle and gets into the proper pursuit angle.

The Sam (offside OLB), reading his initial key (setback), blitzes the offside D gap and is responsible for picking up (#3) if the setback runs a pattern. When there is no pattern from #3, the Sam drops into the secondary and looks to help with coverage.

DIAGRAM 6-9

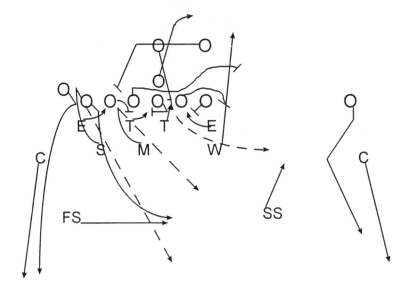

The Mike blitzes the offside B gap and runs into either the offside tackle or the pile created by the setback blocking the offside E. In either case, the Mike is out of position to make the play and he, like the Sam, drops into the secondary to help with coverage.

The Will (playside OLB), seeing the offside guard cross the Spot, is responsible for #3 to the play side. Since there is no possible #3 to the play side, the Will blitzes the C gap. From this point, the Will plays the Waggle in the same manner as in the Base 4–3, illustrated in Diagram 6-5.

The SS (playside S) covers #2 (the fullback) with Man-to-Man coverage.

The FS (offside S) covers the tight end with Man-to-Man coverage.

Both the playside C and the offside C cover #1, to their side, with Man-to-Man coverage. (Diagram 6-9)

THE WAGGLE TO THE TIGHT-END SIDE

Base 4–3 with Green Coverage

Secondary strength is declared to the slot side of the formation.

The strongside E (offside E) attacks the tight end and reads the inside move of the tight end as an attempt to block inside on the Sam. The E gets a good piece of the tight end and steps with his outside foot and turns to the inside looking for a kickout block by the playside guard. When the E sees and feels the attempted hook block by the playside guard, he fights through the block and fights to keep outside leverage. The E, recognizing the hook block, *does not attempt to wrong shoulder the block*. The E is the key defender in stopping the Waggle to the tight-end side. The E *must* maintain outside leverage on both guards and force the quarterback to pull up.

The strongside T (playside T) attacks the playside pulling guard but is blocked by the playside tackle. The T fights through the face of the tackle and gets into the proper pursuit angle.

The weakside T (offside T) attacks the center and is blocked by the center. Like the playside T, the offside T fights through the face of the blocker and gets into the proper pursuit angle.

The weakside E (offside E) attacks the offside tackle as the tackle attempts to cut off the E. The E fights through the face of the tackle and gets into the proper pursuit angle.

The Sam (playside OLB), after reading his key (setback) and the Spot, identifies the Waggle. Since the secondary declared strength to the slot side, the Sam cannot blitz and is responsible for the flat area to the tight-end side. The Sam covers the fullback as the fullback attacks the flat.

The Mike recognizes the action as Waggle. The Mike turns and looks for the slot running a crossing pattern. The Mike gets under the crossing

DIAGRAM 6-10

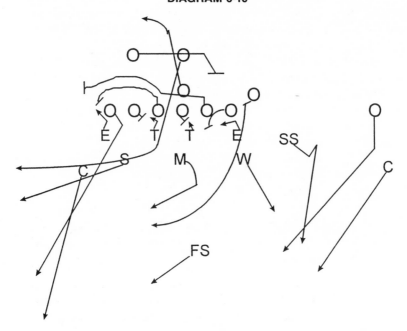

pattern to prevent a completion to the slot. The Mike continues to drop to keep a void area from developing between himself and the FS and giving the slot a location for catching the ball.

The Will (offside OLB), reading the Waggle, drops toward the curl area and undercovers the post route by the split end.

The SS (playside S), from his alignment close to the slot, begins his drop to the curl area but watches the setback (faking Sweep) for a flare or screen route. Seeing the direction the quarterback is taking and no possible pass threat by the setback, the SS drops straight back and looks to help in the secondary.

The C (offside) drops to the deep outside one-third zone and covers the split end running the post route.

The C (playside) drops to the deep outside one-third zone and covers the corner route by the tight end. (Diagram 6-10)

The Base 4–3 with Green coverage is certainly not the best of the three defenses versus the Waggle to the tight end. There is not enough pressure on the quarterback, and the SS is wasted in coverage.

Split with Orange Spy Coverage

The strongside E (playside E) gap charges the D gap and, upon recognition of Waggle, attacks the quarterback. From his outside-in posi-

DIAGRAM 6-11

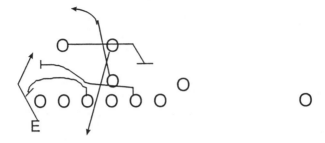

tion, the E can either avoid the block of the offside pulling guard or attack the block and force a quick Pullup by the quarterback. (Diagram 6-11)

The strongside T (playside T) gap charges the playside B gap. When quick enough, the T beats the down block of the playside tackle and disrupts either the playside pulling guard or the offside pulling guard. When not quick enough to completely avoid the block of the tackle, the E does get into the backfield and, often, tackles the quarterback for a significant loss. When the E forces a quick Pullup by the quarterback, the playside T is the defender who has the best chance of getting to the quarterback.

The weakside T (offside T) gap charges through the offside A gap. Like the playside T, if the offside T is quick enough to beat the blocker (center), he is in position to make a great play on the quarterback.

The weakside E (offside E) attacks the offside B gap. The offside tackle gets a piece of the E but not enough to keep the E from getting penetration. The E, seeing the offside pulling guard, follows the guard and, if the E can beat the block of the setback (faking Sweep), he often makes a big play on the quarterback. The possibility of a big play by the offside E is greatly enhanced when the onside E forces the quarterback to pull up. (Diagram 6-12)

DIAGRAM 6-12

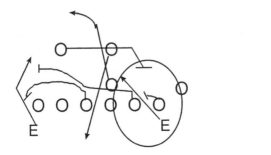

The Sam (playside OLB) is responsible for #2 to the play side. When the Sam notices the fullback coming through the playside A gap, he covers the fullback with Man-to-Man coverage.

The Mike recognizes the Waggle to the tight-end side. The Mike knows that #1 and #2 to both sides of the formation are covered and also knows that #3 to the offside is being covered by the blitzing Will. This leaves the Mike responsible for #3 to the play side. Since there is no possibility of a #3 to the play side, the Mike can blitz the quarterback and become an additional pass-rusher. The C gap normally opens outside the down block of the playside tackle on the playside T. Mike "Shoots" the C gap and can be in great position to sack the quarterback.

The Will blitzes the offside C gap and checks the setback (faking Sweep) for a flare or screen route. If the setback did not pick up the offside E, the setback attempts to block the Will.

The SS (offside S) covers the slot (#2) with Man-to-Man coverage.

The FS drops into the deep middle zone and stays deeper than the slot (#2 offside) running a crossing route. The FS is also aware of the split end (#1 offside) running the post route.

Both C's are in Man-to-Man coverage, covering the #1 to their side of the formation. (Diagram 13)

DIAGRAM 6-13

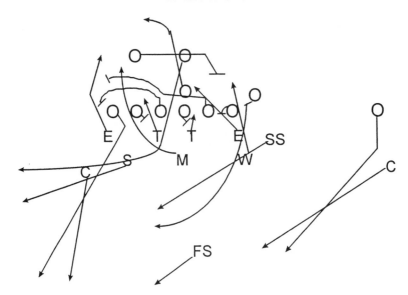

Key Blitz with He-Man Coverage

The strongside E (playside E) employs his slant to the near eye of the playside tackle. The playside tackle is stepping to the inside to down block the playside T. The playside guard attempts to hook the E and the E fights to keep outside leverage on the hook blocker. The E *does not attempt to wrong shoulder the block of the guard.* The E attacks the attempted kickout block by the offside pulling guard. When the E beats the block of the playside guard and forces a block by the offside guard, he has done a good job.

The strongside T (playside T) slants to the center and easily beats the attempted cutoff block by the playside tackle. However, the fullback, protecting the playside A gap, tries to block the T and keep him from getting to the quarterback. The T fights to the play side of the fullback's block and gets into the proper pursuit angle. By forcing the fullback to block, the T eliminates a possible receiver.

The weakside T (offside T) gap charges through the offside A gap. When the offside T is quick enough to beat the blocker (center), he is in position to make a great play on the quarterback coming in behind the pull of the offside guard. (Diagram 6-14)

The weakside E (offside E), versus a slot, slants to the near eye of the slot. The E gets a piece of the slot and disrupts the slot's route. Once the E recognizes Waggle to the tight-end side, he gets into his proper pursuit angle.

The Sam (playside OLB), seeing the offside guard cross the Spot, is responsible for #3 to the play side. Since there is no possible #3 to the play side, the Sam is available to blitz the D gap and become the outside pass-rusher.

The Mike blitzes the offside B gap and runs into the offside tackle. Once the Mike recognizes the Waggle, he drops into the secondary and tries to help with coverage.

DIAGRAM 6-14

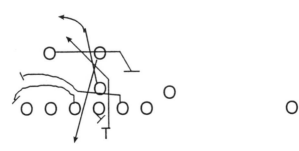

DIAGRAM 6-15

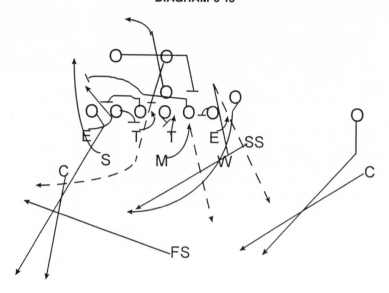

The Will (offside OLB), reading his initial key (setback), blitzes the offside D gap and is responsible for picking up (#3) if the setback runs a pattern. When there is no pattern from #3, the Will drops into the secondary and looks to help with coverage.

The FS (playside S) covers #2 (the fullback) with Man-to-Man coverage.

The SS (offside S) covers the slot (#2) with Man-to-Man coverage.

Both the playside C and the offside C cover #1, to their side, with Man-to-Man coverage. (Diagram 6-15)

KEY POINTS TO STOPPING THE WAGGLE TO THE SPLIT-END SIDE

Base

1. The weakside E (playside E) must keep outside leverage on the attempted hook block by the playside guard.
2. The Mike must locate the tight end as soon as he realizes the Waggle is being executed.
3. The Will must quickly identify the Waggle and attack the quarterback.

Split

1. The weakside T (playside T) must beat the block of the playside tackle and force the fullback to block him, to eliminate a possible receiver.
2. The Mike must recognize the Waggle and blitz as quickly as possible.
3. The Will has to get quick pressure on the quarterback.

Key Blitz

1. The Will must analyze quickly and get quick pressure on the quarterback. The Will is the only outside pass-rusher.
2. Excellent Man-to-Man coverage must be employed because there is not much pressure being exerted on the quarterback.

KEY POINTS TO STOPPING THE WAGGLE TO THE TIGHT-END SIDE

Base

1. The strongside E (playside E) must keep outside leverage on the attempted hook block by the playside guard.

Split

1. The strongside E (playside E) must get good pressure on the quarterback.
2. The Sam must be aware of #2 (fullback) and pick him up immediately.
3. When the strongside T (playside T) beats the block of the playside tackle, he is in position to make a great play.

Key Blitz

1. The Sam must analyze quickly and get quick pressure on the quarterback. The Sam is the only outside pass-rusher.
2. Excellent Man-to-Man coverage must be employed because there is not much pressure being exerted on the quarterback.

Chapter 7

Defending the Belly Pass and Counter-Bootleg

This chapter discusses the Belly Pass and Counter-Bootleg. For the sake of consistency, the wing formation is employed with wing motion. This is the same formation used in Chapter 4 where the Belly and Counter plays are covered. As in Chapter 4, the secondary changes the strength call with the wing motion, and the split-end side of the formation becomes the strong side.

BELLY PASS

Unlike the Waggle, the Belly Pass is not a misdirection passing play. The pass is executed to the side of the full backfield flow. Like the Waggle, the Wing-T makes use of various pass patterns when employing the Belly Pass. In this text, the following basic Belly Pass patterns are described and defended.

- Split End — Out Route
- Setback — Flat Route
- Tight End — Crossing Route

Base 4—3 with Green Coverage

The strongside E (offside E) attacks the tight end and reads the inside move of the tight end as an attempt to block inside on the Sam or release for a pass. The E gets a good piece of the tight end, steps with his outside foot, and turns to the inside, looking for a kickout block by the playside guard or a back. When the E sees no block coming, he gets into his trail mode and is picked up by the offside tackle who is cup blocking. When the E realizes it is a pass, he gets into the proper pursuit angle.

The strongside T (offside T) attacks the offside guard and the guard blocks the T as the guard cup blocks to protect the offside. The T fights through the face of the guard and attempts to attack the quarterback.

The weakside T (playside T) charges the center as the center attempts to protect the playside A gap from penetration. The center delays the charge of the offside T enough for the playside tackle to block inside and block the T. The T fights through the face of the tackle and tries to get to the quarterback.

The weakside E (playside E) recognizes the inside move by the tackle. The E steps with his outside foot, and his shoulders become nearly perpendicular to the LOS. The E is looking for a Trap by the guard. The E sees the playside guard attempting to hook him and the E fights to keep outside leverage on the blocker. When the E does a good job, he remains outside the playside guard and forces the wing (motion) to block him. When the scenario occurs, the playside E has done a very good job.

The Sam (offside OLB), reading his key, begins executing his Hitman technique. When he recognizes a pass, the Sam drops back and under-covers the tight end at the start of the crossing route. Hopefully, the Sam recognizes the pass soon enough to get a hit on the tight end and disrupt the tight end's pattern. Seeing no receiver coming to the offside, the Sam continues to flow through the secondary toward the play side.

The Mike reads the setback step to the weak side. The Mike steps to protect the playside B gap. When the Mike recognizes Belly Pass, he drops back and undercovers the crossing route by the tight end. When the offside E and the Sam do not get a good piece of the tight end, and the Mike does not recognize Belly Pass quickly enough, the tight end finds a void area between the Mike and the SS (becoming the FS with wing motion) and is open for a reception. (Diagram 7-1) A good hit on the tight end by the offside E and the Sam is very important to stopping this play.

The Will, seeing only one back (fullback) attacking the playside B gap, knows the play is either Option or Belly Pass and not Belly. The Will, upon recognition of Belly Pass, drops toward the curl area. It is the Will's responsibility to get between the quarterback and the split end running the out route. Seeing no curl route by the split end, the Will continues his sprint to the outside, anticipating the out route. (Diagram 7-2)

The SS (offside S), on the change of strength, becomes the FS and begins rotating into the deep middle one-third zone. The SS views the tight end's crossing route and keeps the tight end in front of him.

The FS (playside S), on the change of strength, becomes the SS and goes through the curl area to the flat area. Seeing the setback's flat route, the FS comes up and covers the route. The FS stays off the receiver in an

DIAGRAM 7-1

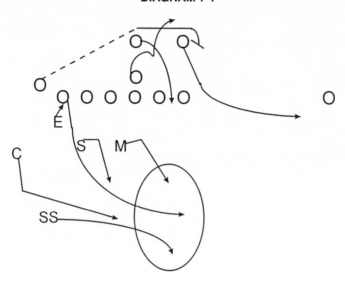

attempt to "Bait" the quarterback into throwing to the setback. When the ball is thrown, the FS steps up for an interception or pass breakup. If the setback does catch the ball, the FS crushes the receiver.

The C (offside C) drops to the deep outside one-third zone. When the C sees no receiver in his zone, and no receiver who could attack his zone, he flows to the play side. Remember, no secondary defender ever "covers grass."

DIAGRAM 7-2

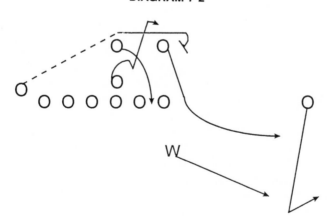

DIAGRAM 7-3

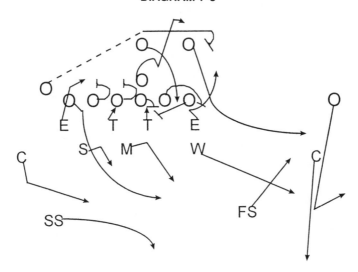

The C (playside C) drops to the playside outside one-third zone and looks for the split end to run an out-and-up route. (Diagram 7-3)

When the ball is thrown, *every defender flies to the ball*. This includes the defensive linemen.

Split with Orange Spy Coverage

The strongside E (offside E) gap charges through the strongside D gap. His charge actually takes him away from the play. When the E sees backfield action going to the weak side, he assumes his trail technique and is cup blocked by the offside tackle. When the E realizes it is a pass, he gets into the proper pursuit angle.

The strongside T (offside T) executes his gap charge through the offside B gap. Like the offside E, the charge of the T takes him away from the play. The T, on recognition of full backfield flow to the weak side, works toward the play side and is picked up by the offside guard who is cup blocking on the offside. When the T realizes it is a pass, he gets into the proper pursuit angle.

The weakside T (playside T) gap charges the playside A gap. The center steps to cut off the T and set the T up for the down block by the playside tackle. Once the center sets up the T, the center checks for any penetration in the offside A gap. When the T is quick enough to beat the block of the center, he puts himself in excellent position to sack the quarterback. The T has to recognize pass as quickly as possible and not tackle the fullback, thinking the fullback has the ball.

DIAGRAM 7-4

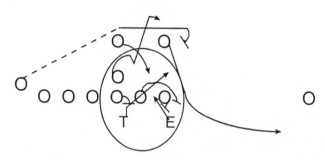

The weakside E (playside E) fires through the playside B gap. The playside tackle, stepping to the inside, makes contact with the E and attempts to pin the E to the inside. The E gets hit by the offside tackle but should be able to get some penetration into the backfield. By being forced to block the E, the playside tackle cannot get down on the playside T. This allows the T a much better chance to get into the backfield for an attack on the quarterback. (Diagram 7-4) Unlike the Waggle to the split-end side, the Belly Pass does not have the fullback protecting the playside A gap before releasing for a pass.

In this chapter, as in other chapters, it is understood that all three linebackers execute their normal key and Spot reads. All descriptions of linebacker action in this chapter occur after their reads.

The Sam (offside OLB), with wing motion, no longer has the tight end with Man-to-Man coverage. The Sam becomes the Hitman and flows toward the play side. Upon recognition of Belly Pass, with no #2 releasing to the offside, the Sam is out of position to effectively blitz the quarterback. The Sam drops into the secondary and looks to help another defender.

DIAGRAM 7-5

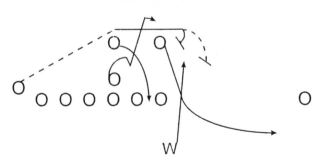

The Mike, initially reading Belly, steps toward the play side. On a pass in Man-to-Man coverage, the Mike is responsible for #3. Upon identification of the Belly Pass, the Mike looks for the fullback. When the fullback executes a pass route, the Mike takes him with Man-to-Man coverage. When the fullback is blocking, the Mike makes sure the fullback is not delaying to release late for a pass before he goes through the fullback to blitz the quarterback. The Mike rarely, if ever, gets to the quarterback. The Mike spends too much time analyzing the possibility of the fullback releasing for a pattern. This eliminates the Mike as an effective pass-rusher but also prevents the fullback from running a route not covered by a defender.

The Will (playside OLB) blitzes the C gap and either beats the block of the wing or, at least, attacks the block of the wing and forces the quarterback to pull up. Under no circumstances can the Will permit the wing to block him to the inside and allow the quarterback to get outside and attack the corner. (Diagram 7-5)

The SS (offside S), on the change of strength, becomes the FS and begins rotating into the deep middle one-third zone. The SS views the tight end's crossing route and keeps the tight end in front of him. For the SS, it is the same as Green.

The FS (playside S), on the change of strength, becomes the SS and is responsible for #2. When the safety sees the flat route by the setback, he comes up and covers the setback with Man-to-Man coverage.

Both C's cover #1, to their side, with Man-to-Man coverage. (Diagram 7-6)

DIAGRAM 7-6

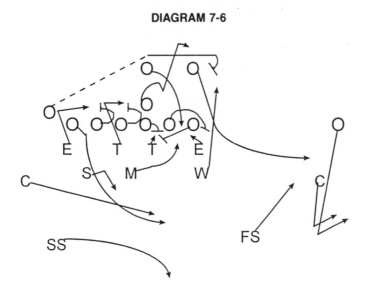

Key Blitz with He-Man Coverage

The strongside E (offside E) slants to the near eye of the offside tackle. The tackle steps into the B gap and then cup blocks to the offside and picks up the slanting E. The E fights through the face of the tackle and attempts to rush the passer. When the ball is thrown, the E gets into the correct pursuit angle.

The strongside T (offside T) slants to the near eye of the center. The offside guard steps into the offside A gap, gets a piece of the T, and pushes the T into the pile created by the center attempting to block the playside T. The T may be able to squeeze into the backfield between the offside guard and center but is too late, and too far from the quarterback, to force a quick pass or a sack. However, when the quarterback is forced to pull up, the offside T does have a chance to make a great play.

The weakside T (playside T) fires through the playside A gap. If the T is quick enough to beat the center's block, chances are the down-blocking tackle will not be able to block the T. Again, since the fullback does not protect the playside A gap, the T does have a good shot at getting a sack or, at least, of forcing a very quick pass.

The weakside E (playside E) slants to the near eye of the playside guard. The playside tackle, stepping to the inside, has a much better chance of blocking the slanting E than he has of blocking a gap-charging E. However, as in Split, the tackle has no chance of blocking the playside T, and this gives the T a good opportunity for a great play on the quarterback.

The Sam (offside OLB) assumes his Hitman technique and slowly flows toward the Belly fake. Upon recognition of Belly Pass, with no #2 releasing to the offside, the Sam is out of position to effectively blitz the quarterback. As in Orange Spy, the Sam drops into the secondary and looks to help another defender.

The Mike, while reading his blitz key, flows to the play side. Mike does not blitz when his key goes to the weak side. He views the fullback in the B gap. If the fullback releases on a route, the Mike picks up the fullback and covers him with Man-to-Man coverage. When the Mike *knows the fullback is blocking and not releasing on a route*, the Mike drops into the secondary and helps with coverage. (Diagram 7-7)

The Will, while reading his blitz key, blitzes the playside C gap. The Will reacts in the same manner as in the Split Front. The Will either beats the block of the wing or, at least, attacks the block of the wing and forces the quarterback to pull up. Under no circumstances can the Will permit the wing to block him to the inside and allow the quarterback to get outside and attack the corner.

The SS (offside S), on the change of strength, becomes the FS and begins rotating into the deep middle one-third zone after checking for a #2

DIAGRAM 7-7

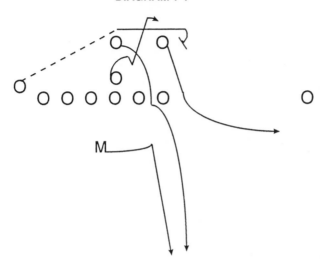

releasing to the offside. The SS becomes a true FS and plays the Belly Pass in the same manner as Green and Orange Spy coverages.

The FS (playside S), on the change of strength, becomes the SS and is responsible for #2. When the safety sees the flat route by the setback, he comes up and covers the setback with Man-to-Man coverage.

The playside and offside C's are in Man-to-Man coverage and cover #1 to their side. (Diagram 7-8)

DIAGRAM 7-8

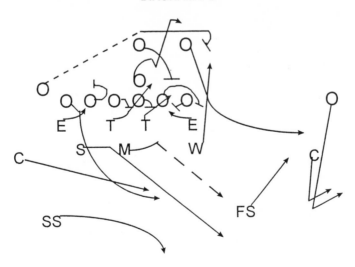

COUNTER-BOOTLEG

The Counter-Bootleg is a misdirection passing play and is similar to the Waggle to the split-end side in this respect. The linebackers, however, see their key, the setback, stepping to the strong side after "rocking" his shoulders toward the weak side. The linebackers also see a blocker (offside tackle) crossing the Spot in the same direction as the setback. Unlike Waggle, the pulling offensive lineman does not cross the Spot opposite the backfield key. Therefore, the defenders initially read the play as HB Counter. The quickness with which the defenders recognize the pass determines how well they can effectively defend against the play.

In this text, the following basic Counter-Bootleg patterns are described and defended.

- Split End — Slant Corner Route
- Fullback — Flat Route
- Tight End — Crossing Route

Base 4–3 with Green Coverage

The strongside E (offside E) attacks the tight end and reads the inside move of the tight end as an attempt to block inside on the Sam or release for a pass. The E gets a good piece of the tight end and steps with his outside foot and turns to the inside looking for a kickout block by the playside guard or a back. The E views the offside tackle crossing the Spot and expects the HB Counter. When the E recognizes Counter-Bootleg, he is too late to effectively rush the passer and he gets into his proper pursuit angle.

The strongside T (offside T) attacks the offside guard and is blocked by the guard. The T fights through the face of the guard and the T tries to rush the passer when he identifies the passing play. When the T is fortunate enough to beat the block of the guard, he meets the setback, faking the HB Counter, in the offside A gap.

The weakside T (playside T) attacks the center and is blocked by the center and the playside guard. The T fights through the face of the guard and rushes the passer.

The weakside E (playside E) attacks the offside tackle and reads his pull toward the strong side. Recognizing the blocking scheme as HB Counter, the E looks for the block by the fullback. When the fullback does not attempt to block the E, the E realizes it is Counter-Bootleg and fights to keep outside leverage on the block of the wing (motion). The play of the E is pivotal to stopping the quarterback.

The Sam (offside OLB), seeing the setback step toward the strong side and the tackle cross the Spot, thinks the play is HB Counter. Once he recognizes Counter-Bootleg, he drops into the secondary to help. The movement of the setback and the tackle crossing the Spot normally takes the Sam totally out of the play. When the Sam does recognize the Counter-Bootleg, he works his way back toward the play side to help in coverage.

The Mike, like the Sam, initially reads the play as HB Counter. Once he recognizes the Counter-Bootleg, the Mike drops and attempts to undercover the crossing route of the tight end.

The Will (playside OLB) begins his Hitman technique, thinking the play is HB Counter. However, once the Will discovers the play is Counter-Bootleg, he blitzes the quarterback and becomes the outside rusher.

Like the Waggle to the split-end side, if the offense changes the basic patterns and has the split end execute a curl instead of a slant-corner route, the split end is open and, on the next play, a different coverage has to be used, or the Will has to be employed in the curl area (his basic Green coverage area of responsibility) and the blitz eliminated.

The SS (offside S), on the change of strength, becomes the FS and begins rotating into the deep middle one-third zone. The SS sees the crossing route by the tight end and keeps the tight end in front of him.

The FS (playside S), on the change of strength, becomes the SS and goes through the curl area to the flat area. Seeing the flat route by the fullback, the FS comes up and covers that route.

The C (offside C) drops to the deep outside one-third zone. When the C sees no receiver in his zone, and no receiver who could attack his zone, he flows to the play side.

The C (playside C) drops to the playside outside one-third zone and looks for the split end running the slant-corner route. (Diagram 7-9)

DIAGRAM 7-9

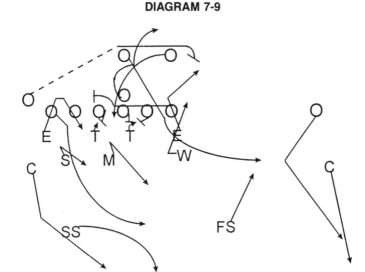

Split with Orange Spy Coverage

The strongside E (offside E) executes his gap charge through the offside D gap. This move takes the E away from the play. When the E realizes the play is Counter-Bootleg, he is too far out of position to put on a pass-rush. The E gets into the proper pursuit angle.

The strongside T (offside T) gap charges the offside B gap. The T is picked up by the offside tackle, who is protecting the offside B gap, and the offside guard blocking to protect his area. The T fights through the block to the play side. However, the T is also too far from the play to be an effective pass-rusher, particularly since the T's initial charge is opposite the direction of the play. Like the offside E, the T gets into his proper pursuit angle.

The weakside T (playside T) fires through the playside A gap. The T is blocked by the center and the playside guard. Unless the T is extremely quick and the center and the playside guard are very slow, the T rarely gets through to get to the quarterback. The T fights through the face of the playside guard and fights to get to the quarterback.

The weakside E (playside E) gap charges the playside B gap. If the playside guard leaves the playside T for the center to block alone, the guard is in position to block the gap-charging E. However, when this occurs, the T has a great chance of beating the center and getting to the quarterback. (Diagram 7-10) When the playside guard does block the T, the E fires into the backfield and either gets to the quarterback or knocks the fullback off his route. The playside E is often the defender who breaks this play. (Diagram 7-11)

The Sam (offside OLB), with wing motion, no longer has the tight end with Man-to-Man coverage. The Sam becomes the Hitman and flows toward the play side. Seeing the pulling playside tackle cross the Spot and the setback coming toward the strong side, the Sam believes the HB Counter is the play. Upon recognition of Counter-Bootleg, the Sam looks for a #2 releasing to the offside (strong side). Unless the setback releases after faking the HB Counter, the Sam has no receiver to cover and the Sam is out

DIAGRAM 7-10

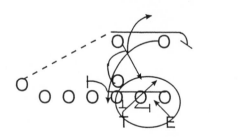

DIAGRAM 7-11

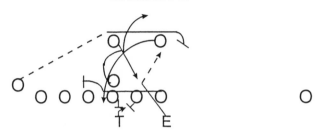

of position to effectively blitz the quarterback. The Sam drops into the secondary and looks to help another defender.

The Mike, initially reading HB Counter, steps toward the offside A gap, his gap responsibility to the strong side. On a pass in Man-to-Man coverage, the Mike is responsible for #3. Upon identification of Counter-Bootleg, the Mike knows there is no possibility of a #3 receiver to either side. This frees the Mike to blitz the quarterback. From his position, the Mike is rarely an effective blitzer unless the quarterback is forced to prematurely pull up and the quarterback cannot quickly find an open receiver.

The Will (playside OLB) blitzes the C gap and either beats the block of the wing or, at least, attacks the block of the wing and forces the quarterback to pull up. Similar to defending the Belly Pass, the Will, under no circumstances, can permit the wing to block him to the inside and allow the quarterback to get outside and attack the corner.

DIAGRAM 7-12

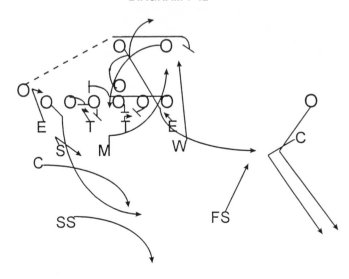

The SS (offside S), on the change of strength, becomes the FS and begins rotating into the deep middle one-third zone. The SS views the tight end's crossing route and keeps the tight end in front of him. For the SS, it is the same as Green.

The FS (playside S), on the change of strength, becomes the SS and is responsible for #2. When the safety sees the flat route being executed by the fullback, he comes up and covers the fullback with Man-to-Man coverage.

Both C's cover #1, to their side, with Man-to-Man coverage. (Diagram 7-12)

Key Blitz with He-Man Coverage

The strongside E (offside E) slants to the near eye of the offside tackle. The tackle, blocking area, picks up the E. The E fights through the face of the tackle and rushes the passer.

The strongside T (offside T) slants to the near eye of the center. The offside guard tries to block the T but can only push the T to the play side. The T has an excellent chance of getting to the quarterback if he can beat the setback filling the offside A gap. The T fights to the play side of the setback and often is the defender who gets to the quarterback. (Diagram 7-13)

The weakside T (playside T) does exactly the same thing in Key Blitz that he does in Split.

The weakside E (playside E) slants to the near eye of the playside guard. If the playside guard leaves the playside T for the center to block alone, the guard is in position to block the slanting E. However, when this occurs, the T has a great chance of beating the center and getting to the quarterback. When the playside guard does block the T, the E slants to the area vacated by the playside guard and either gets to the quarterback or knocks the fullback off his route. Because the slant is slower than the gap

DIAGRAM 7-13

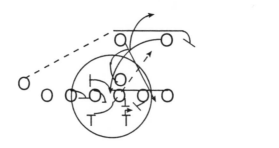

DIAGRAM 7-14

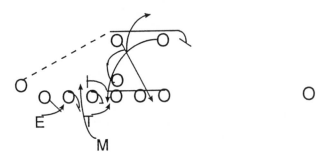

charge and the gap charge allows the penetration into the backfield, the slanting E has less of a chance of making a great play than the gap-charging E.

The Sam (offside OLB), reading his key (setback), blitzes the strong-side D gap. This charge takes the E away from the play. When the Sam recognizes Counter-Bootleg, he tries to get into the secondary to help. The E rarely has any effect on the play.

The Mike blitzes the offside B gap. The Mike normally gets through the gap created by the offside guard blocking inside on the offside T and the offside tackle blocking the offside E. The playside pulling tackle is left to block the Mike. The Mike fights through the tackle but, like the Sam, rarely has an effect on the play. (Diagram 7-14)

DIAGRAM 7-15

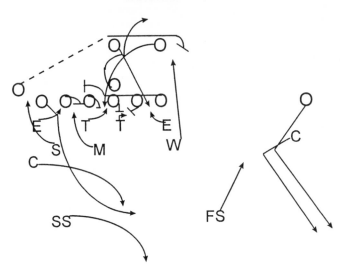

The Will (playside OLB), having no #3 release to his side, blitzes the playside C gap. The Will attacks or avoids the block of the wing (motion) and forces the quarterback for a sizable loss.

The SS (offside S) rotates into the deep middle zone and keeps the tight end, executing the crossing route, in front of him. While dropping, the SS looks for a possible #2 releasing to the offside.

The FS picks up #2 and covers the fullback with Man-to-Man coverage.

Both the playside C and the offside C cover #1, to their side, with Man-to-Man coverage. The playside C covers the split end and the offside C covers the tight end. (Diagram 7-15)

KEY POINTS TO STOPPING THE BELLY PASS

Base

1. The playside E must recognize the attempted Hook block by the playside guard and keep outside leverage on the block.
2. The Sam and the offside E must get a piece of the tight end to disrupt his crossing route.
3. The Mike needs to recognize Belly Pass quickly enough to undercover the crossing route by the tight end.
4. The Will must recognize only one back attacking the playside B gap.

Split

1. When quick enough, the playside T can beat the block of the center and have an excellent chance to sack the quarterback.
2. The Mike must cover the fullback (#3) if he runs a route, or attack the fullback if he blocks. When the Mike is sure the fullback is blocking, the Mike must fight through the fullback's block and attack to the quarterback.
3. The Will needs to keep outside leverage on the block of the wing. The Will can never allow the wing to block him inside.

Key Blitz

1. The Mike must use his Blitz Peel technique if the fullback releases on a route.
2. The FS has to come up quickly enough to effectively cover the setback.

KEY POINTS TO STOPPING THE COUNTER-BOOTLEG

Base

1. The playside E must keep outside leverage on the block of the wing.
2. The Mike has to quickly recognize the Counter-Bootleg and undercover the tight end running a crossing route.
3. The Will must analyze the play quickly and blitz the quarterback.

Split

1. When the playside guard blocks the playside T, the playside E has a great chance of sacking the quarterback.
2. The blitzing Will must keep outside leverage on the block of the wing.
3. The quicker the Mike recognizes Counter-Bootleg, the better are his chances of being effective blitzing the quarterback.

Key Blitz

1. The blitzing Will must keep outside leverage on the block of the wing and, at least, force the quarterback to pull up.

Chapter 8

Defending the Sprint-Out Pass

Most teams execute Sprint-Out passes with the quarterback opening to the side of the play. Wing-T Offenses often have the quarterback reverse pivot to the side of the play. The reverse pivot complements the other parts of the offense. Whether the quarterback employs an open step or a reverse pivot, the defense handles the Sprint-Out in the same way. Although most Wing-T Sprint-Out passes are executed to the split-end side of the formation, there are certain times when Sprint-Out passes are executed to the tight-end side of the formation.

SPRINT-OUT PASS TO THE TIGHT-END SIDE

When a defense employs a great deal of Green coverage to the side of a slot formation, the Wing-T offensive coordinators often employ Sprint-Out passes to the tight-end/setback side of the formation. Although the possible routes vary greatly, in this discussion the following routes are employed:

- Setback — Flat Route
- Tight End — Corner Route
- Slot — Crossing Route
- Split End — Deep Post Route

Base 4—3 with Green Coverage

Versus the slot formation, the secondary declares strength to the slot side of the formation.

The strongside E (playside E) attacks the tight end and attempts to disrupt his outside pass release. After making contact with the tight end and recognizing a passing play, the E attacks the blocking fullback and keeps outside leverage on the blocker. The E does not want to allow the quarterback to get outside and attack the corner.

The strongside T (playside T) attacks the playside guard and keeps outside leverage while fighting to get to the quarterback. With no defender attacking the playside C gap, the playside tackle is free, after checking the C gap, to help the guard with the T.

The weakside T (offside T) attacks the center. The center punches the T toward the offside guard as the center steps to protect the playside A gap. The offside guard, stepping to protect the offside A gap, hits the T and pushes him toward the center. The center, finding no defender in the playside A gap, cup blocks and picks up the T. The T fights through the face of the center and attempts to rush the passer.

The weakside E (offside E) attacks the offside tackle. The E fights through the face of the tackle and rushes the passer. The E is also mindful of his trail technique and looks for a reverse.

The Sam (playside OLB) reads pass as he sees his setback key sprint to the outside and the quarterback open or reverse pivot and become a passer to the strong side. The Sam, knowing that in Green coverage there is no flat coverage away from the secondary strength and there is no curl area to a single tight-end side of a formation, picks up the setback on the setback's flat route. (Diagram 8-1)

The Mike, recognizing Sprint-Out pass to the strong side, opens to the tight-end side and sprints in the same direction as the quarterback. As the Mike sprints toward the play side, he is aware of the crossing route by the slot and he undercovers that route.

The Will (offside OLB), reads Sprint-Out pass away and begins to drop toward his curl area. Seeing the post route by the split end, the Will undercovers that route. Since there is no possibility of another receiver coming into the curl area, the Will stays with the split end. If the quarterback does decide to throw back to the split end, he must throw the ball over the Will and in front of the C. The Will and the C have the split end bracketed.

The SS (offside S), seeing the inside release by the slot, must still check the offside flat before dropping into the secondary to help. The SS knows there is no need to cover the flat when there is no possibility of the area being attacked by a receiver. The SS never "covers grass."

DIAGRAM 8-1

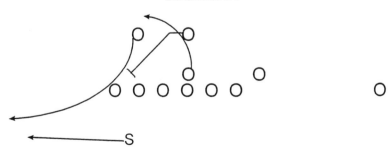

DIAGRAM 8-2

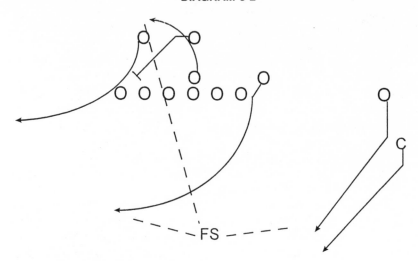

The FS (playside S) drops into the deep middle zone and keys the quarterback. The FS is aware of the slot executing the crossing route and also aware of the split end running the post route. Even though the offside C is helping with the post route by the split end, the FS cannot run with the slot and disregard the split end's route. However, since the quarterback is sprinting to the tight-end side, the chances of the quarterback throwing back to the split end are slim. (Diagram 8-2)

DIAGRAM 8-3

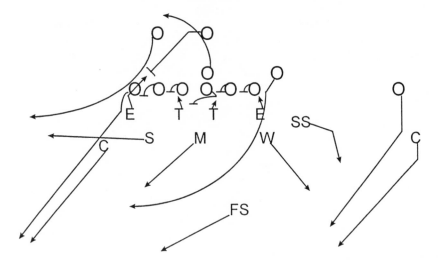

The C (playside C) drops to the deep outside zone and covers the corner route by the tight end.

The C (offside C) drops into the offside deep one-third zone and covers the split end's post route. When the C realizes there is no other possible receiver who can threaten his area, the C stays with the split end and helps FS with the coverage. (Diagram 8-3)

Split with Orange Spy Coverage

The strongside E (playside E) gap charges the D gap. This puts the E in a good position to attack the fullback but allows the tight end to release without having his route disrupted. The E attacks the fullback and forces the quarterback to pull up. The E cannot allow the fullback to block him to the inside.

The strongside T (playside T) charges into the playside B gap. The playside guard initially hits the T, and the playside tackle, seeing no defender attacking the playside C gap, helps the guard with his block. The T fights through the face to the tackle, attempting to rush the passer.

The weakside T (offside T) fires into the offside A gap. The center punches the T toward the offside guard as the center steps to protect the playside A gap. The offside guard, stepping to protect the offside A gap, hits the T and pushes him toward the center. The center, finding no defender in the playside A gap, cup blocks and picks up the T. The T fights through the face of the center and attempts to rush the passer. Unless the center and/or the offside guard expect a quick penetrating charge by the T, the T may be able to beat their blocks and put an effective rush on the quarterback. However, rarely does the T beat the blocks.

The weakside E (offside E) gap charges the offside B gap. Since the offside guard is concentrating on the weakside T, the playside tackle is left to block the gap-charging E. Unless the offside tackle is quick enough to stop the charge of the E, the E can get into the backfield and put an effective pass-rush on the quarterback. If the playside E is effective in forcing the

DIAGRAM 8-4

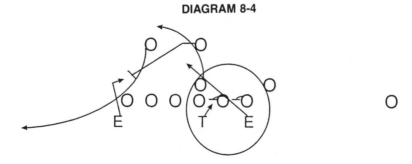

DIAGRAM 8-5

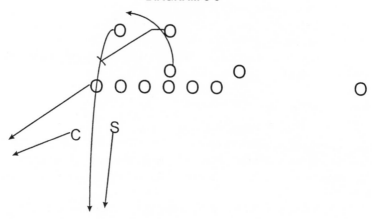

quarterback to pull up, the offside E has a good shot at getting to the quarterback and making a great play. (Diagram 8-4)

The Sam (playside OLB), seeing his key (setback) step to the strong side, is responsible for #2 in Orange coverage. The Sam covers the setback's flat route. If instead of the setback running a flat route and the tight end executing a corner route, the two receivers run a crossing route, the Sam takes the inside receiver and the playside C would take the outside route. (Diagram 8-5)

The Mike sees his key step toward the strong side. Versus a pass, the Mike is responsible for #3 to either side. Since there is no possibility of a #3

DIAGRAM 8-6

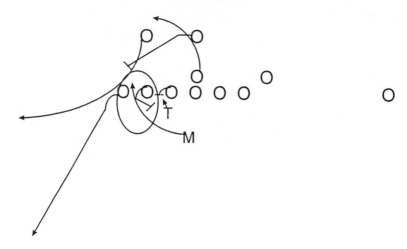

DIAGRAM 8-7

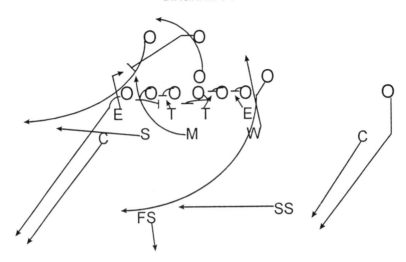

to either side, the Mike is free to blitz. The Mike looks for the first open gap to the play side and blitzes that gap. When the playside tackle blocks the playside T, the C gap is open and the Mike blitzes that gap, often sacking the quarterback. (Diagram 8-6)

The Will (offside OLB) blitzes the C gap. The Will is often left unblocked but is normally too far from the play to effectively pressure the passer. However, if the Will is very quick in blitzing and analyzing the play, he can be efficient in getting to the quarterback, especially when the quarterback is forced to pull up.

The SS (offside S) covers the slot with Man-to-Man coverage. The SS knows the FS is in the deep middle and will give the SS help over the top.

The FS covers the deep middle one-third area as though the coverage is Green.

Both the playside C and the offside C cover #1, to their side, with Man-to-Man coverage. (Diagram 8-7)

Key Blitz with He-Man Coverage

The strongside E (playside E) slants to the near eye of the tackle. The playside tackle, stepping through the C gap, makes contact with the E but does not get outside the E. The E fights to keep outside leverage on the tackle's block and rushes the passer. When the E is effective in quickly getting off the tackle's block, the fullback is forced to block the E. When this occurs, the Sam has an excellent chance of sacking the quarterback. (Diagram 8-8) When the tackle is capable of blocking the E and keeping

DIAGRAM 8-8

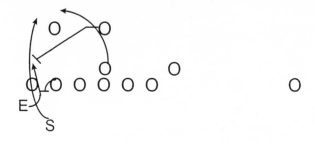

him out of the backfield, the fullback can block the Sam and the chances of the defense sacking the quarterback are minimized.

The strongside T (offside T) slants to the near eye of the center. The playside guard gets a piece of the T and pushes the T into the playside A gap where the center picks him up after the center punches the offside T to the offside guard. The T, initially slanting away from the play, fights off the block of the center and toward the quarterback.

The weakside T (offside T) fires into the offside A gap. The center punches the T toward the offside guard as the center steps to protect the playside A gap. The offside guard, stepping to protect the offside A gap, hits the T and pushes him toward the center. The center, blocking the playside T, cannot step back and help with the offside T. Therefore, the offside guard is left with the job of blocking the T by himself. The offside T, with a quick charge, often beats the offside guard and gets to the quarterback. (Diagram 8-9)

The weakside E (offside E), versus a slot, slants to the near eye of the slot. The E attempts to get a piece of the slot and disrupt his route. (Diagram 8-10) The E rushes the passer but must remain aware of his trail responsibility.

The Sam (playside OLB), reading his setback key, blitzes the playside D gap. When the fullback is forced to block the E, the Sam has a clear shot

DIAGRAM 8-9

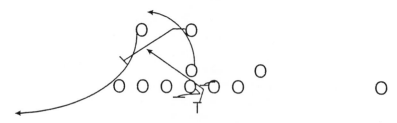

DIAGRAM 8-10

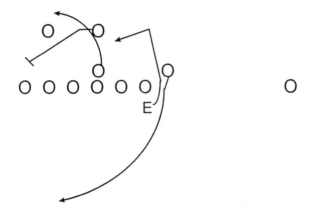

at the quarterback. When the playside T can block the E and keep him out of the backfield, the fullback blocks the Sam. The Sam cannot allow the fullback to block him to the inside.

The Mike, reading his setback key, blitzes the playside B gap. The playside guard, after getting a piece of the slanting playside T, is in position to pick up the blitzing Mike. The Mike keeps outside leverage on the guard's block and fights to get to the quarterback.

The Will (offside OLB) assumes his Hitman technique. When the Will recognizes Sprint-Out pass and sees no possibility of a #3 releasing to his side, he drops into the secondary to help with coverage.

DIAGRAM 8-11

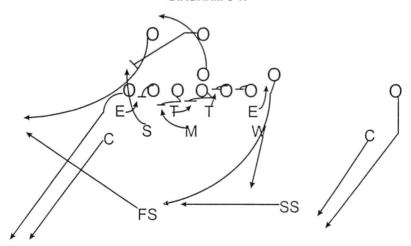

The SS (offside S) covers the slot with Man-to-Man coverage.

The FS, with a #2 releasing to his side, covers the flat route of the setback. This becomes true Man-to-Man coverage with no Free Safety in the deep middle zone. Even though #1 and #2 are not executing crossing routes, the Inside-Outside rule could be employed in this situation. The C could take the setback (outside receiver) and the FS could cover the tight end (inside receiver).

Both the playside C and the offside C cover #1, to their side, with Man-to-Man coverage. (Diagram 8-11)

SPRINT-OUT PASS TO THE SPLIT-END SIDE

The favorite Wing-T formation for a Sprint-Out pass is the slot formation; the pass is executed to the slot/split-end side of the formation. For our discussion, the following routes are employed:

- Setback — Check, Away
- Tight End — Crossing Route
- Slot — Flat Route
- Split End — Curl Route

Base 4–3 with Green Coverage

The strongside E (offside E) attacks the tight end and disrupts the tight end's inside move. At this point, the E does not know if it is a pass or a run. After making contact with the tight end, and recognizing a passing play, the E rushes the passer and is picked up by the offside tackle. The E goes through the face of the tackle as he rushes the quarterback.

The strongside T (offside T) attacks the offside guard and fights through the guard's attempted cup block.

The weakside T (playside T) attacks the center and is blocked by the center. The T fights to keep outside leverage on the center as he rushes the passer. When the playside guard finds no defender to block in the playside B gap, the guard can slide back to help the center with the T. When the guard does step back to help the center, the T attacks the guard and fights through his face to the quarterback.

The weakside E (playside E) attacks the playside tackle and maintains outside leverage on the block. Once the E recognizes the passing play, he fights off the tackle's block and attacks the blocking fullback. The E keeps outside leverage on the fullback as he rushes the passer. The E is the outside contain and he cannot allow the quarterback to get outside and attack the corner. (Diagram 8-12)

DIAGRAM 8-12

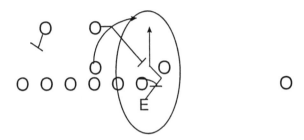

The Sam (offside OLB) recognizes Sprint-Out pass to the split-end side and, hopefully, can get a piece of the tight end releasing to the inside. Knowing the offside flat is not covered in Green coverage and there is no curl area to the single tight-end side of the formation, the Sam picks up the setback executing an away route. With no other possible threat to his area, the Sam can continue to drop with the setback's flat route.

The Mike, recognizing Sprint-Out pass to the weak side (weak side to the front and strong side to the secondary), opens to the slot side and sprints in the same direction as the quarterback. As the Mike sprints toward the play side, he is aware of the crossing route by the tight end and he undercovers that route.

The Will (playside OLB), upon recognition of Sprint-Out pass to his side, sprints to the curl area. While sprinting to the curl area, the Will looks at the split end to determine if the split end is executing a curl route. When the Will recognizes the curl route, the Will covers the route and discourages the quarterback from throwing to the split end.

The SS (playside safety), recognizing Sprint-Out pass to his side, sprints through the curl area to the flat area. By going through the curl area, the SS gives the Will time to get to the area to cover the curl route by the split end. The SS then comes up and covers the slot's flat route.

The FS (outside S) drops into the deep middle zone. The FS is aware of the tight end running a crossing route and the FS stays over the top of the route while the Mike plays under the route.

The C (offside C) drops into the offside deep outside zone and sees the setback running an away route. The C stays in his zone and remains over the top of the setback's away pattern. The setback is bracketed by the C and the Sam.

The C (playside C) drops into the playside outside one-third zone and looks for a deep pattern by the split end or a possible wheel route by the slot running a flat route. (Diagram 8-13) When there is no deep route by the split end or wheel route by the slot, the C steps up to a position over the top of the

DIAGRAM 8-13

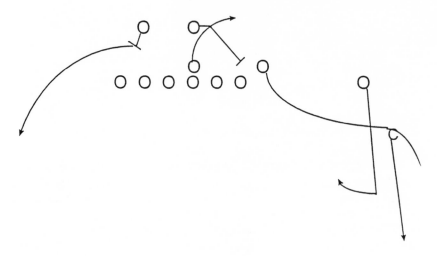

curl route. However, because of the possibility of the wheel route, the C hangs back and is a factor on the curl route only after the split end catches the ball. (Diagram 8-14)

Split with Orange Spy Coverage

The strongside E (offside E) gap charges the D gap. The E's charge takes him away from the play. The E, upon recognition of Sprint-Out pass away, rushes the passer but remains aware of his trail responsibility and

DIAGRAM 8-14

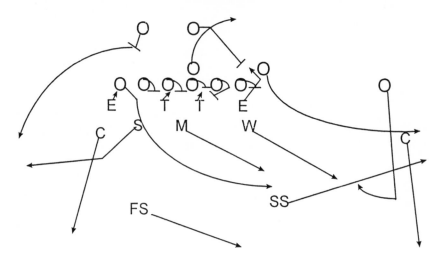

looks for a reverse. The E is picked up by the offside tackle and the E fights through the face of the tackle.

The strongside T (offside T) executes his gap charge through the offside B gap. This charge also takes the T away from the play. When the T realizes the play is a Sprint-Out to the weak side, the T fights through the offside guard who is attempting to block the T.

The weakside T (playside T) charges through the playside A gap. The center steps to prevent penetration through the A gap and makes contact with the T. When the playside guard steps to pick up the gap-charging playside E, the T has a good chance of beating the center to the play side and getting into the backfield.

The weakside E (playside E) gap charges through the playside B gap. The playside guard picks up the E. Like the T, if the guard single blocks the E, the E has an excellent chance of beating the guard to the play side and getting into the backfield.

The Sam (offside OLB) sees his key run the away route to his side. Since the setback is #2, the Sam looks to pick him up with Man-to-Man coverage. However, this is a situation when the Inside-Outside rule is applied (Chapter 2). The Sam takes the tight end running the crossing route and the C picks up the setback executing the away route. (Diagram 8-15)

The Mike steps to the play side on Sprint-Out pass action to the weak side, after he sees his key, the setback, step to the offside. In Orange Spy coverage the Mike is responsible for #3 to either side. Since there is no possibility of a #3 to either side, the Mike is free to blitz. The Mike blitzes the first open gap to the play side and attacks the quarterback.

The Will (playside OLB) blitzes the C gap. The playside tackle attempts to pick up the Will but is often too slow after slightly reacting to the inside move of the playside E. The Will fights through the blocking fullback and

DIAGRAM 8-15

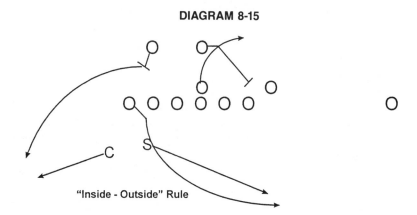

"Inside - Outside" Rule

DIAGRAM 8-16

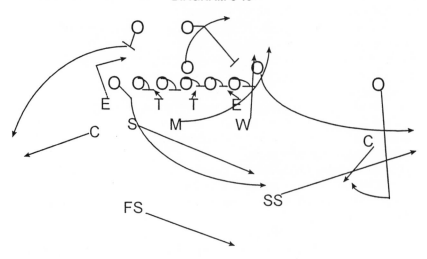

attacks the quarterback. The Will can never allow the fullback to block him to the inside. The Will either sacks the quarterback or forces him to pull up.

The SS (playside S) covers the slot with Man-to-Man coverage.

The FS (offside S) drops into the deep middle one-third zone and plays in the same manner as Green coverage.

The C (offside C) plays Inside-Outside rule with the Sam, and the C covers the setback running the away route. (Diagram 8-15)

The C (playside C) covers the split end with Man-to-Man coverage. (Diagram 8-16)

Key Blitz with He-Man Coverage

The strongside E (offside E) slants to the near eye of the offside tackle. The offside tackle picks up the E and the E fights through the face of the tackle as the E rushes the quarterback.

The strongside T (offside T) slants to the offside eye of the center. The offside guard, initially stepping to the offside A gap, gets a piece of the T. With the center stepping to block the playside T, there is a slight gap that develops between the offside guard and the center. When the offside T is quick enough to recognize this gap and quick enough to beat the full effect of the offside guard's block, he can get into the backfield and effectively rush the passer. (Diagram 8-17)

The weakside T (playside T) does exactly the same thing in Key Blitz that he does in Split.

DIAGRAM 8-17

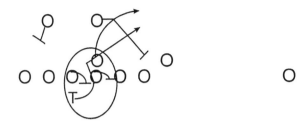

The weakside E (playside E), versus a slot, slants to the near eye of the slot. The E attempts to get a piece of the slot and disrupt his route. The E rushes the passer as the playside tackle tries to block him. However, the E keeps outside leverage and, hopefully, forces the fullback to block him.

The Sam (offside OLB), seeing his key step to the offside, blitzes the offside D gap. This move takes the Sam away from the play. Upon recognition of Sprint-Out pass away, the Sam drops into the secondary to help with coverage.

The Mike, seeing his key step to the offside, blitzes the offside B gap. Like the Sam, the blitz takes the Mike away from the play. Once the Mike recognizes Sprint-Out pass away, the Mike drops into the secondary to help with coverage.

The Will (playside OLB), reading Sprint-Out pass to his side, is responsible for #3. Since there is no possibility of a #3 releasing to his side, the Will blitzes the open D gap. When the playside E has done a good job by forcing the fullback to block him, the Will is free to the quarterback. (Diagram 8-18)

The SS (playside S) covers the slot with Man-to-Man coverage.

The FS (offside S) is responsible for #2. However, this is a situation when the Inside-Outside rule is applied (Chapter 2). The FS takes the tight end running the crossing route and the C picks up the setback executing the away route.

DIAGRAM 8-18

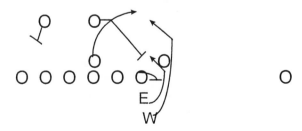

DIAGRAM 8-19

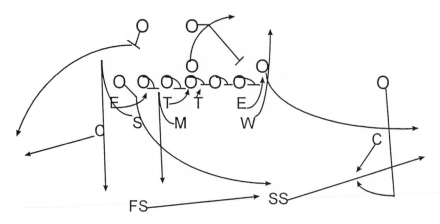

The C (offside C) takes the setback executing the away route and employs the Inside-Outside rule.

The C (playside C) covers the split end with Man-to-Man coverage. (Diagram 8-19)

KEY POINTS TO STOPPING THE SPRINT-OUT PASS TO THE TIGHT-END SIDE

Base

1. The strongside E must keep outside leverage on the blocking fullback.
2. The Sam, realizing there is no flat coverage away from the secondary strength call in Green Coverage, has to cover the setback in the flat.
3. The Mike has to become aware of the crossing route being executed by the slot.

Split

1. From his outside leverage position, the strongside E must force the quarterback to pull up.
2. The Sam, being responsible for #2, must pick up the setback. The Sam must be aware of a crossing route between the tight end and the setback and be ready to apply the Inside-Outside rule.
3. The Mike must quickly recognize Sprint-Out pass and realize he is to blitz.

Key Blitz

1. The blitzing Mike must keep outside leverage on the block of the playside guard and effectively blitz the passer.
2. The FS and playside C must remain aware of the possibility of an Inside-Outside rule being needed.

KEY POINTS TO STOPPING THE SPRINT-OUT PASS TO THE SPLIT-END SIDE

Base

1. The weakside E must keep outside leverage on the blocks of the playside tackle and the fullback.
2. The SS must flow through the curl area to buy time for the Will to get there to cover the curl route by the split end.
3. The playside C cannot come up to cover the curl route due to the possibility of a wheel route by the slot.

Split

1. The Sam must pick up #2 (the setback) executing the away route and the Sam must be aware of the Inside-Outside rule.
2. The Will has to analyze Sprint-Out pass very quickly and blitz as hastily as possible.
3. The offside C has to be aware of the possible application of the Inside-Outside rule.
4. The Mike has to recognize Sprint-Out pass and blitz.

Key Blitz

1. The Will has to blitz as quickly as possible.
2. The FS and offside C have to be ready to apply the Inside-Outside rule.

Epilogue

The discussion in this book makes it apparent that, at times, one of the three defensive schemes is better against a particular offensive play than the other two. Although one scheme may be better than the other two, all three are effective against all Wing-T plays. As strongly stated in the beginning of this document, the real *key* to defensive success is **DISGUISE.** *Never allow the offense to know which scheme is coming.*

All three defensive schemes can be executed from the Base alignment, the Head-Up alignment, or any combination of the two. Employing only the Base alignment, or various alignments, prohibits the quarterback from getting any valid presnap read and eliminates the possibility of a quarterback audible to take advantage of any perceived weakness in any of the three defensive schemes.

I have truly enjoyed writing this text. I hope you have enjoyed reading it and have gotten much usable knowledge from it.

FOOTBALL'S MODERN 4-3 DEFENSE, Bob Kenig
($18.00)

This book presents a comprehensive guide to football's most popular defense. Coach Kenig, a successful coach and multi-book author, offers a step-by-step look at every aspect of this defense, including invaluable chapters showing the 4-3 against the game's most popular offenses.

Contents

Getting Ready to Employ the 4-3 Defense
Selecting Personnel for the 4-3 Defense
The 4-3 Tackles and Ends
The 4-3 Linebackers
The 4-3 Secondary in Cover 2
4-3 Front Variations and Line Stunts
4-3 Secondary Variations
The 4-3 Blitz Package
The 4-3 Nickel Package
The 4-3 Vs. the Wing-T Sweep and Trap
The 4-3 Vs. the Single-Back, Drop-Back Passing Game
The 4-3 Vs. the I-Option Play
The 4-3 Vs. the Counter-Gap Play
The 4-3 Vs. the No-Back, Three-Step Passing Game

FOOTBALL'S MODERN ZONE BLOCKING, John Durham
($13.00)

This timely guide explores the technical basis of the foundation for modern zone blocking and describes the fundamentals necessary for offensive line play from the ground up. More important, it details all the aspects of team blocking and how to teach and refine it to run some of the popular offensive power plays.

The corollary to zone blocking is gap blocking. This book explains the concept of gap blocking and how it is implemented. These gap schemes are the basis of counter plays. Variations of gap blocking and zone blocking are also defined.

Coach Durham discusses zone blocking for pass protection for the drop-back, movement, and misdirection passing games. He examines in detail the blocking schemes for the counters to the passing game—many kinds of misdirection passes, draws, and screens.

(See last page for order form.)

FRITZ SHURMUR
Defensive Coordinator
GREEN BAY PACKERS

COACHING THE DEFENSIVE LINE (video) ($30.00)

Fritz Shurmur, with demonstrations by Gilbert Brown, Bob Kuberski, and Gabe Wilkens, has produced an exceptional teaching video for both coaches and players. This 50-minute instructional video covers all of the fundamentals for teaching or becoming an excellent defensive lineman.

COACHING THE DEFENSIVE LINE (book) ($16.00)

"I'm glad Fritz Shurmur is on my side. He's an excellent teacher who also knows how to motivate. His books on defensive football must be part of every coach's library. Fritz is one of the best coaches I've ever worked with. Coaching the Defensive Line is a must read."

> Mike Holmgren
> Head Football Coach
> Green Bay Packers

"Coaching the Defensive Line is another must read for all coaches and fans of fundamental football. It's a terrific tool for coaches at any level. From basic fronts, proper stance and drills, to the mental preparation needed, Fritz Shurmur covers all there is to know. This book is the 'Bible' of defensive line play."

> Matt Millen
> TV Football Analyst
> Fox Sports

COACHING TEAM DEFENSE, Second Edition ($12.00)

Considered to be one of the best books ever written on football defense, this excellent guide provides a solid fundamental approach to understanding and executing the basic concepts of team defense. It is about coaching defense with the basic idea of getting as many as possible of the 11 players on the field to the ball. This book is intended for the football coach at any level of play and regardless of coaching experience or philosophy.

THE EAGLE FIVE-LINEBACKER DEFENSE ($12.00)

Fritz Shurmur presents a unique and innovative defensive scheme which is based on solid principles, techniques, and drills that are applicable to any defensive plan at any level of play. This unique defensive concept allows coaches to attack today's wide-open offenses rather than having to react.

(See last page for order form.)

COACHING THE DEFENSIVE BACKFIELD, Greg McMackin ($12.00)

This book is a thorough study of all the fundamentals, techniques, and drills you will need to produce a successful secondary. Coach McMackin, the defensive coordinator of the Seattle Seahawks, helps you prepare your secondary through a complete plan concerning skills, techniques, and game-like drills that will enable you to produce a fundamentally sound and aggressive defensive backfield.

FOOTBALL'S EXPLOSIVE MULTI-BONE ATTACK, Tony DeMeo ($12.00)

Coach DeMeo, who is presently the head coach at Washburn University, is widely recognized as one of the most innovative offensive coaches in football today. His Multi-Bone combines the explosiveness of the Veer, the power of the I, the deception and misdirection of the Wing-T, the ball control of the Wishbone and the wide-open play of the Pro Drop-back Passing game. This book shows you how to tie together the best of these offenses into one easy-to-learn package.

COACHING RUN-AND-SHOOT FOOTBALL, Al Black ($12.00)

This unique guide presents an exciting attack that can enhance your present offense or stand alone. Coach Black, a successful 30-year coaching veteran whose career includes a very impressive 149-41-2 high school record, gives you all the run-and-shoot pass routes, plus blocking schemes, a complementary offense, a one-back running game, and much more.

DEFENSING THE RUN AND SHOOT, Bob Kenig ($12.00)

The defensive system in this book employs both odd and even fronts, which are skillfully utilized with man-to-man, zone and combination defenses. The book also provides you with an extensive blitz package, plus an invaluable chapter that shows you how to disguise the defenses. Coach Kenig recently completed his latest book, *Stopping the Wing-T With the 4-3 Defense*, available from Harding Press ($15.00).

(See last page for order form.)

HARDING PRESS, INC.
P.O. BOX 141
HAWORTH, N.J. 07641
(201) 767-7114
FAX: (201) 767-8745
hardingpress@earthlink.net

ORDER FORM

# of COPIES	TITLE	TOTAL PRICE

Postage & Handling: SUBTOTAL_____

Order	U.S.	Outside U.S.	
Under $25.00	$ 3.50	$ 8.25	NJ Residents –
$ 25.00 – $ 49.99	$ 5.25	$11.00	Add 6% Sales Tax _____
$ 50.00 – $ 74.99	$ 6.75	$12.25	
$ 75.00 – $ 99.99	$ 8.00	$13.25	P & H _____
$100.00 – $149.99	$ 8.75	$14.00	
$150.00 – $199.99	$ 9.50	$15.00	TOTAL _____
$200.00 +	$10.25	$15.50	

EACH ORDER MUST BE ACCOMPANIED BY CHECK, M.O., P.O., or CREDIT CARD info

COACH'S NAME _____

ADDRESS _____

_____

CITY _____ **STATE** _____ **ZIP** _____

PHONE # (_____)_____
          area code

MASTERCARD/VISA: _____
                    Card #   Exp. Date

_____
          Signature